Labyrinth of Love

Moving Closer

Andrea Maude

BALBOA.
PRESS
A DIVISION OF HAY HOUSE

Balboa Press books may be ordered through booksellers or by contacting:

Balboa Press
A Division of Hay House
1663 Liberty Drive
Bloomington, IN 47403
www.balboapress.com.au
1 (877) 407-4847

Because of the dynamic nature of the Internet, any web addresses or
links contained in this book may have changed since publication and
may no longer be valid. The views expressed in this work are solely those
of the author and do not necessarily reflect the views of the publisher,
and the publisher hereby disclaims any responsibility for them.

The author of this book does not dispense medical advice or prescribe the use
of any technique as a form of treatment for physical, emotional, or medical
problems without the advice of a physician, either directly or indirectly. The
intent of the author is only to offer information of a general nature to help
you in your quest for emotional and spiritual well-being. In the event you use
any of the information in this book for yourself, which is your constitutional
right, the author and the publisher assume no responsibility for your actions.

Any people depicted in stock imagery provided by Thinkstock are models,
and such images are being used for illustrative purposes only.
Certain stock imagery © Thinkstock.

Print information available on the last page.

ISBN: 978-1-4525-2736-9 (sc)
ISBN: 978-1-4525-2737-6 (e)

Balboa Press rev. date: 02/26/2015

Introduction

Labyrinth—a guided path to our source? What resonates at the centre is the elusive question. With a strong desire to move closer to my truth, a search begins to unravel the mysteries within.

I share with you an insight into a part of my labyrinth. "Who am I?" you may ask. I am one of many tasked with offering some spiritual insights as to why we are struggling more than we have to. I have been guided to share this personal story to help provide a level of understanding that we can all move into a new way of living. There are some embarrassing stories and some heartfelt explanations on how I found my true self once I released my past. This enabled me to progressively travel forward on my path with love and joy.

We all have little gems to share to encourage others to actively search for purpose and enjoy this journey. It's a choice to make the most of this fantastic opportunity in our play we call life. In this mortal stage of the eternal labyrinth, it is up to each and every one of us to value this time. It's about learning and sharing knowledge. To also help anyone who could do with some unconditional love, material support, or emotional understanding.

It's nice when we get the foresight to call on higher powers in everyday situations, not just when things get so dire in illness or mental turmoil. There is increasing awareness surfacing everywhere of spiritual assistance most of us can't see; however, the things we put down to an amazing coincidence are often fully aided by energies desperately trying to get our attention.

It took me over twenty years to take the time to listen. However, I am now an awakened New Zealander who has been tapped on the shoulder—or should I say taken over the edge of this reality?—to undeniably know there is something more. As we try to grasp the concept that we are all at different stages in our evolutionary education, I encourage you to take the time to explore your innate gifts which are guiding you home.

Awaken

Our planet is changing
So what do we know?
Spirit is knocking
To put on a show.

They're raising us up
To let us all see,
Our spiritual truth
So we can break free.

Meeting ourselves,
The dark and the light.
Integrating them both
To give up the fight.

The glowing truth shines
With no real remorse.
Embracing the new
By connecting our source.

We're coming together
Our next stage forward,
With kindness to others;
A mutual reward.

We collectively share
What's found to be real.
The love that we give
Is how we can heal.

Chapter 1

August 1, 1975, was a good day for my entrance. I was the second-born child of parents Cindy and Phil Maude; my sister Julie had been born three years earlier. In every sense, I had picked a family that would provide me with solid boundaries and a comfortable upbringing. My first name was nearly Louise, but with the family dog named Louie, Louise got relegated to a middle name, and Andrea it was to be. As a child, I was described as unknowingly funny yet publicly shy. It's amazing for me now to think back and review some of the spiritual signs that occurred when I was so young. These insights have undoubtedly led me to keep searching and sharing the possibilities of being fully connected to the all that is.

My mum, Cindy, an attractive lady, has always been a planner. She is always looking five years ahead, and she thrives on being the in-control caretaker. Mum grew up in a pink house on Auckland's North Shore. The house colour was chosen by her father, who had a fondness for the local sugar refinery, which was painted pink. Being the youngest in her family, she became very close to her mum, my nana Oli. I have only recently found out that my grandfather Bill, who passed away when I was a toddler, was a spiritualist who helped perform healings and regularly assisted in negative-energy-clearing sessions. Mum had not been interested in these things while growing up; however, we are now both curious to know what Granddad really knew about life and the hereafter.

Phil, my dad, who is no longer with us, was a rebel in an Australian Catholic family in his youth. As a family man, he was generally happy to come along for the ride. Living with three strong-willed women, he was definitely outnumbered. This may be why we always had a token male pet; unfortunately for Dad, this was often a neutered poodle. We tried to offset the breed's feminine stereotype with the last dog we acquired by giving him a masculine name: Jake. Dad had a passion for listening to music; he could completely tune out the world around him when he popped his headphones on and relaxed with his selected sounds. In more spiritual discussions with Mum, she advised he did have a connection with his spirit guide. I have an inkling Dad and I shared previous life experiences, as we felt comfortable in our silence together.

Julie, my sister and a great friend, has assisted my learning process in this lifetime. She has come to my rescue on so many occasions from childhood dramas and travelling mishaps to failed relationships and life-changing moments. Back when we were going through puberty, she was a great sense-check when I needed to make sure things were "normal" with my physical body. This was obviously prior to the Internet. Over the years, we explored many places of the world together. One of Julie's gifts is a heavenly singing voice. On our worldly travels, I fondly remember the angelic sound of her voice when she broke into song whilst sitting in an acoustic marble-and-stone Turkish steam room, prior to us receiving our scrub-down.

Growing up, I recall some memorable family tales. One that is imprinted firmly in my mind is a visit from some of our Australian relatives. Dad was one of the six children in his Catholic-raised family, so I have cousins galore, as most of his brothers and sisters had reproduced well. Some of these relatives were heavily involved with the entertainment industry. It wasn't the cool musician kind with concerts and fame. No, it was more like the off-the-wall, creative, circus kind: trampolining, water-stunt

events, and fire blowing were all part of the act. One year, they tried to teach us some of their tricks of the trade. However, Julie and I never could quite master the unicycle, and Dad tried his hand at fire blowing with disastrous results. Simple instructions were given for him to hold a fire accelerant in his mouth while dipping his arm in a protective liquid. Then he was to blow some flames up his drenched limb, all to create the illusion that he was a fire-breathing hero. Events often go quite pear-shaped when one has consumed a few too many beers before attempting feats like this. With a dramatic change in wind, his dragon breath got out of control and singed off his silver comb-over that he had cultivated over many years. Our trampolining lessons also went into a shock situation when our two-metre-square yellow trampoline was being used for stunts. When everyone was trying to do tricks simultaneously, I decided it was way too intense, so I took action to get off. Unfortunately, I was bounced headfirst straight into the unprotected springs. Blood started gushing from my highly vascular head. Julie rushed me to Mum, who took me into the bathroom to assess the damage. Looking at myself in the full-size wall mirror, all I could focus on was my favourite dress with beautiful yellow flowers, which was now covered in blood. The pain was put on hold while I assessed the damage to the dress. As Mum couldn't stop the bleeding, I was taken to accident and emergency, while Christmas dinner turned to mush. As much as these little episodes make life what it is, these tales are not really what I want to describe in detail. The accounts I wish to impart are my acquired experiences with energetic entities that are closer to us in this physical reality than we may choose to believe.

Our family home on Carlisle Road in Auckland's North Shore was a red-and-white, brick two-storey house with a pottery business in the basement. It was perched at the top of a generous sloping quarter-acre section. The kitchen was at the back of the house. It was a functional space with a door that had the standard etchings of children's growth rates—ours and local friends'.

The cream-and-green linoleum flooring was a fashion statement for the times, and I used to sit on the U-shaped bench top and watch Mum peel, chop, and cook. On the baking days, I would sit waiting patiently for the sugar-and-egg-white-laden beater heads to be handed to me so I could lick them clean of the meringue mixture. The kitchen was semi-open to a large dining room that had varnished wooden floors and a dark, wood, oval table. This room was also home to a day couch, a dog bed, and the family piano. I can't neglect the radio-cassette player that sat on top of the piano surrounded by various music tapes. This room was north facing, so it was bright and lively, and the orange net curtains just added to the seventies charm. It was a great situation, having both parents at home to spend time to nurture and teach two girls the ins and outs of growing up. Most of the daytime, while Dad was downstairs glazing various dishes and painting shapely cups with gold rims, the girls hung out, often with Nana Oli.

Nana Oli was a retired seamstress, and with her passion for sewing, Julie and I were lucky enough to have wardrobes full of the most gorgeous handmade dresses. Nana's life was full of amazing events that encompassed the developing times. Being born on 12/12/1912, she lived through periods of scarcity and struggle. This must have given her immense emotional strength, as the Nana I knew and loved so much had an amazing calm and giving approach to life. It was fantastic that she was always close at hand while I was growing up.

My childhood days seemed so long, like time could just be put on hold while my imagination seemed to pave the way ahead. The biggest decision of the day was choosing a location for the sheeted fort to be built. It was under the dining room table, in the jungle gym outside, or between the two single beds in my room. Once the bed-linen hut was set up, my orange plastic furniture and pink tea set were laid out for entertaining my various guests. Julie, Panda, and my doll Crystal would regularly partake in the festivities.

Mum also planned weekly shopping trips into town; this was before every suburb had its own mall. The Farmers Trading Company department store was the main destination. At Christmastime, the excursions were even more of an event, as for all of December, the store had a large Santa erected on the outside of the very tall building. He was fully equipped with a winking eye and a large finger that moved in a manner to entice us closer. Julie and I had the tiresome task of tagging along with Mum and Nana, shopping each floor yet knowing the rooftop playground would be our reward.

One particular year, we were in the clothing department where Mum and Nana were rummaging the discount baskets looking for bargains. I was extremely bored, so I decided to get onto a plinth, where some nicely dressed mannequins were showcasing their attire. I struck a pose and practiced my stillness. Two shoppers proceeded to walk past. When one of them grabbed the skirt of my homemade dress, she fanned it out to admire the detail my nana had put into the trim. My plastic persona dissolved when I flinched, and one of the ladies started screaming as her mannequin came to life. When many people gathered to see what the commotion was, I quickly ran back to hide behind Mum. After the woman had restored her regular heart rhythm, she came over to where I was cowering and started chatting with Mum and Nana. On finding out Nana had made the dress I was modelling, she congratulated her on some beautiful sewing. This small token of admiration of Nana's work made her day, and luckily, the lady saw the funny side of my antics.

After that debacle, we finally made it to the rooftop playground. However, Mum always made us have some sustenance before play, so we made our way to the adjacent tearooms. My usual lunch was a mince pie that had to be drowned in tomato sauce. This was the good old days where there was no fear of unhealthy fats or undesirable preservatives. After the pie was dissected and Mum was satisfied I had eaten enough, we were allowed to go to the massive toy-laden arena. As eager as I was to get there, I wasn't really an automatic joiner. As a true little sister, I would follow Julie's cue on what to play on. I will never forget the feeling of immense electricity in the air produced by so many high-pitch voices, and I now wonder how many other children there had "imaginary" friends.

I can't quite recall my first encounter with Jennifer. I think Julie had started school so my playmate was gone. Sitting in the kitchen, our green pullout table was up and I was seated in a high, plastic-coated, cane-woven stool, and I asked Mum to set another place as I had someone joining me for lunch. Her hair was really long and her tastes were the same as mine. We chatted for a while as we ate rolled luncheon sausage and sauce, quite content with my new friend; physically visible or not, the connection was real. There were play dates where we made feijoa stew with hundreds and thousands, which was compulsory for Mum to sample. Some days I was just pleased to know that she was with me. Over thirty-five years ago, it seems as real today as it was then, when I take my memories and feelings back to those moments. When it was my turn to start school, interaction with Jennifer faded, as I had solid friends to make.

Sherwood Primary School gave me a few spiritual clues that I unwittingly collected in my childhood. In my first year, I was quite nervous to be landed with so many strangers, yet I always managed to make a few core friends. I was perceived as quiet; however, I had one teacher that really brought out the best in me. She taught me the art of visualisation, which is often a key to discovering some hidden insights. The time a fundamental piece of my puzzle was found was an overcast and bleak day. One of the teachers had requested I take a note over to another teacher who was working in the library. I had to walk through A-block courtyard and around to an area that was often a wind trap. I recall seeing tiny whirlwinds swirling up the dust and debris across the concrete like nature's self-cleaning device. The airy feeling of the powerful skies above and the deserted playground made me tense; nonetheless, I reluctantly proceeded to complete my task. On nearly reaching the library door, I looked down, and just as it seemed to be placed in my path on purpose, this labyrinth stencil made from a brass kind of metal drew me closer. I picked it up and was fascinated with the trinket's circular perimeter. Its quadrant-patterned path detailed on its interior just seemed so familiar. At the age of five, I had things in my subconscious that would eventually drive me to search for more truth.

One year this school tried to introduce religious instruction classes. I had an awareness of what religion was, even though my family were not regular churchgoers. We did say grace when we ate dinner. The only two prayers my family used were "For what we are about to receive, may the Lord make us truly thankful. Amen." My addition to this was "Rub-a-dub-dub, thanks for the grub, yeah, God." I felt rather proud reciting grace each night. Mum had told me some Bible stories as I was often asking questions and trying to work out how this heaven thing worked. One afternoon our family was having a ceremony in the garden for our recently deceased pet and I casually asked, "Why are we burying Mitzy down there when heaven is up there?" while pointing skyward. My parents didn't really have any answers I was satisfied with, so my next question was directed at Nana Oli. "When we bury you in the garden, what tree will we plant on top?" Silence ensued and a change of conversation quickly occurred.

When the religious instruction classes started at school, all of the children were gathered in an open-plan classroom. The three instructors were on a raised area looking down upon us in a somewhat dictatorial manner. I think their intentions were good—to give us a level of biblical understanding—except there was no openness to explore our questions for alternative meanings that could be gained from some of these tales. When I asked if pets go to heaven, there was an outright no. I thought something was a bit off and I wasn't quite willing to settle for that response.

That night I went home and asked Mum if I could have a note to excuse me from these lessons. She was comfortable with this, as she could feel my distress. I was one of a few children who went to the library to read when these classes were on. The other kids that were exempt from these lessons had opposing family religious beliefs. I was really the only child that was sitting on the fence, so to speak, hoping to work it out for myself. Over the weeks, the group going to the library started to get bigger. I am unsure if this was due to the fact that others found a way to skip this class or that the teachings became more negative in approach for which they didn't want to be a part of.

Years later I actually asked Mum if I could go to Sunday school with a friend's family who was heavily into the church. They too had some limited views, but I took on board some of the aspects of the written texts they shared. I mainly enjoyed watching how their community interacted with each other. Most of their congregation supported each other in their tough times and genuinely cared for those in need. I had a hunger to learn more, which sadly faded when boys and acting cool became more important. However, this didn't matter, as these early symbolic experiences started the path of my colourful voyage that lay ahead in my quest for finding spiritual wisdom.

Invisible Friendship

New beginnings
And wanting to share,
Longing to include her
In the big world fair.

Internal play
Using slow time,
I thought I had lost
Those memories of mine.

Not from here, no;
A magical place,
Touching my heart
And filling that space.

Joining me
At my table for two,
Having some lunch
Is what we would do.

Not seen by eye
But felt by me,
Jennifer was
My gift energy.

I didn't stop
The belief in my friend
Until time sped up
To hasten its end.

Chapter 2

The physical body: love it or hate it. We have to learn how to adapt to the fact that this is the vehicle we are using for this human experience. As I mentioned, it was nice to have a sister to chat with about bodily functions when I wanted to establish answers on why things had to be the way they were. I guess for most of us who had siblings, bath time was often when more questions arose. I have to laugh at some of the stunts Julie and I tried when we were quite young. One bath time, we decided to try to swap tongues. Little did we know we were kissing in a way we would only learn about in many years to come. With our observations, we established that both of us had the same bits so we didn't really know how boys were different. My young, inquisitive mind wasn't only focused on the physical body, as there were so many other questions to life. Could animals talk to each other? Where do you go if you don't go to heaven? Why did I often feel like I was falling in my sleep? Why did Nana need to dye her hair purple? Why do old men have big ears? These were quite big questions for anyone to answer.

Going back to the day when I was quite young, I discovered something peculiar in my mouth which was somewhat puzzling at the time. One Sunday family drive, Julie and I were sitting in the back seat with the dog perched between us as we giggled with the naughtiness of a game I made her engage in. The rules of the contest were to pass the dog's leather lead through his legs for the other person to take hold of it. Then with a mini tug of war, the aim of the game was to pull the opponent's hand into the dog's wet willy. Slightly distracted, she got me, and not only did I get wee juice on my hand, but I was preoccupied with this awful thing accumulating in my mouth. "Mum, what is this in my mouth?" I squealed. I was handed a hanky to offload the offending foreign matter and I returned it to her for investigation, yet nothing could be seen. "There's more!" I shouted. I tried repeatedly to show her something for which she just couldn't ascertain. She leaned over from the front passenger's seat to have a good look in my mouth, with the announcement that all she could see was spit. "Spit," I said. Finding out that I had been swallowing the stuff for my entire life to date was a complete shock. How could I have not known it was in there this whole time? Now that swallowing had been brought to my attention, my thoughts on having to do this consciously, all of the time, was quite worrying. I pondered this for the journey until I was briefly distracted with another game of "pass the lead through the poodle." Then swallowing once again got relegated to a subconscious task, rarely to be thought of again. But what else did I not know I was doing?

The fascination with learning about the whys of the human body kept the questions flowing for my parents. We often had older visitors come to the house and I would often look at their wrinkled faces and think, *What caused all of those lines?* The fascination of the phenomenon of old men's ears getting bigger and bigger as they aged also intrigued me. *Dad's are pretty big already, so how big can they actually get?*

I remember at a very young age jumping into my parents' bed and bugging Mum until she woke. I would draw paths on her face with my index finger and she would take part in the ritual of pretending to bite it when I got too close to her mouth. I would also draw pictures and letters on her back for which she had to guess what I was trying to illustrate. One morning while playing these games, Dad returned from having a shower. Dad was usually quite discrete on dressing when Julie and I were in their bedroom. One morning Mum asked him a question when he was towel-less and facing the wardrobe. He turned around momentarily, forgetting I was in their bed. That was the day I saw something I had never seen, and before Dad could do anything, I leaned over. "Ding a bell," I said while whacking his male appendage. Then I turned back to Mum and continued to play. No explanation was needed, as I always knew Dad was different.

On growing up, Julie was more of a peacemaker than a challenger. As a young, happy-go-lucky personality, she joyfully embraced new things and people. She would sing and perform and would talk to anyone. I, on the other hand, was reserved and untrusting, often having bouts of anger which frequently saw Julie as my punching bag. Where were these deeply contained feelings coming from? I surely had not been conditioned to this in my violence-free family. Were these past hurts at five years of age? I certainly didn't remember any. I guess we all have times where the mind's programming tests the boundaries and learning life's lessons takes you on a journey to discover who you are.

Julie's nature as the trustworthy giver was tested when the pressures of primary school got to her. We were both at the same school and it was a year that the game marbles made a comeback. Julie and I had been bought various kinds of glass marbles years earlier, but we had not really taken much care of this precious commodity. Once the craze hit school, it was all on; marble mania had begun. I tried to go through my drawers to find the marbles I knew I previously owned, to no avail. I found this quite strange, so I enlisted Mum's help to do some digging into the matter. "Julie, have you seen Andrea's marbles?" *(This is the glass kind, not my mental marbles that were at risk later on in this story.)* Silence from Julie, then a hesitant no came from her lips. Julie doesn't lie, so I was advised there was no luck.

I tirelessly searched some more, yet not one marble was found. I knew I previously had various kinds, like Ord's, Milky Ways, and even some Bonkers, but still nothing came from this futile searching. Julie was too quiet. Was guilt making her withdraw? I had to do my own detective work. I snuck into her room and searched under the bed, in the wardrobe, and everywhere until I saw it: a fabric bag hidden under layers of clothes in one of her drawers. The bag was full of my marbles just waiting to be put at risk in playtime gaming. "Mum!" I yelled. "Julie has my marbles." Mum's disappointment in her was evident. I didn't feel good about getting Julie in trouble, but I am sure she was being taught that lies to self-protect out of fear are often short-lived. My frustrations were dissipated when Mum took me shopping and bought me the latest Galaxies. These were a sought-after black marbles set, with various coloured specs that I only dreamed about owning. Strangely enough, once I acquired my own collection, I then wasn't that keen to partake in the madness to put them all on the line to potentially loose them all. I just wasn't a risk taker, so I kept them in a homemade bag Nana helped me make. My marbles—the glass collection and my mental kind—are two things I endeavour to keep for this lifetime.

I had fantastic childhood stability, as we never once moved homes. Mum and Dad worked hard to get us some fun things, which included a swirling slide that went into our para-pool. My parents were a bit slow on the uptake on technology though as spending frivolously on the latest gadget didn't fit with Mum's five-year financial plan. We generally bought technical things years after development, which made me jealous of my neighbour across the street who had the latest soda stream machine, video player, and electronic toys. I also didn't get pocket money so I couldn't save for the things I wanted. In the early days, Julie and I used to work out ways we could earn some simple coin for our candy treats. We would perform shows where we would sing and dance. Synchronised swimming routines were also on the event calendar. The entrance fee to watch these shows was twenty cents, which could buy us a decent amount of sweets back in the day.

However, after various performances, our family audience of three had seen too many shows, so I had to come up with other ideas of gathering some money. My sweet tooth was strong, so the desire to find some other ways of getting lollies was quite compelling. The art of cash collecting went on for quite a few years. It got harder in my preteen years, when I was too young to work and not as cute to put on shows. I had an idea for which I pitched to my friend that lived across the road. The plan was to make a card for our elderly neighbour, in the hope she would give us something for our efforts. Hours of investment went into constructing a beautiful card with glittery pictures and words that were meant to tug at the heartstrings—or should I say purse strings? We went over to her house and she invited us in. "We have made you something, Aunty May." She wasn't really an aunt, as she was nearly the same age as my nana, so I'm not sure where that title came from. On presenting the card, she could see our eager, greedy objective, hoping for a payoff. All of that work with nothing but a thank-you and a call to Mum to advise we were there. We received a stern lecture on our poor choice of funds gathering. I didn't get it. We didn't beg. We didn't even ask for anything. Nonetheless, my key learning from that day was my underlying intentions were off. I was being taught a sense of morals I wasn't yet aware of, and these lessons kept coming.

Being the more self-centred child, I would strategize the path for minimal effort when Julie and I were given shared household jobs. On hanging the washing out, I would sell Julie the concept that I couldn't hang them straight, and to prevent me from getting a growling, she agreed I could just hand her the pegs. I would also skive off at dishes time so I didn't have to start the washing. Drying them, however, was manageable, as I would take so long that assistance would always be given. My world at this time was all about me, until all of a sudden, a surprising thought reversal came one Christmas day. I loved to draw and colour; creating things just seemed to fit with me. I had put a lot of effort into making and sourcing the best Christmas present for each member of my family. It was Christmas Eve when Mum asked if I was excited about getting my Christmas gifts and I replied, "No, I can't wait to give out mine." She nearly fell over as her youngest child was overcome with unselfish desire. *Wow! What a turnaround. Excellent progress*, she thought. My decision-making journey saw many steps forward and backward, and my choices didn't always flow with goodness when mixing with certain friends at intermediate school. But I guess that's what peer pressure and testing the rulebook is all about.

I think I was about twelve when Mum and Dad had a party at home. Socialising was not really my scene. There had been enough manners ingrained in me that I could pass around snacks and be polite. I didn't have the confidence to engage in long, adult conversations though. When the folks were getting merry on alcohol, Julie and I became very bored. For our own entertainment, we dared each other to knock back the dregs of everyone's drinks in the kitchen. Then we spied the Southern Comfort bottle. It was strong but nice and sweet. I took a few swigs. Instant personality transplant! Mum made the statement that she had never seen me so engaged with their guests, dancing and having fun. Mum stopped drinking, which gave her enough time to get sober enough to drive some individual's home. I keenly volunteered to come along for the ride. "Fantastic. I will have company for the return trip," Mum said. Little did she know there would be various pit stops on the return trip for me to relieve myself of the cocktail of spirits I had consumed. So there was another lesson for my collection: alcohol is toxic to the human body! Did I unwittingly create a neurological link that I can become more likeable with alcohol? Answer: yes! Did it take me decades to remember alcohol is a poison? Answer: yes!

Becoming a teenager is a time in life that most of us cringe to think about on reflection. What we have we don't want, and what we don't have are largely the things we desperately desire.

Wishing the pimples would go away and having an urgent need for my womanly period to arrive was not much to ask for. All of my friends had got their cycle, and waiting for mine to arrive each month with not a drop of blood led to so much disappointment. Lying in bed one day and looking at the holly-hobby wallpaper on my bedroom walls, that my parents had promised to replace five years earlier, was still glaring at me like I was a child. The attempt to cover them up with ready-to-roll music posters did make the room a bit more tolerable, but I still didn't have my gift that would see me into womanhood. I am not quite sure what the prompt was, but I decided to ask God for a deal that I hadn't really thought through before I put my request out there. "God, can I get my period when we get some cats?" Oh my goodness. What had I just done? Mum was not a huge fan of cats, so why did I say that? It will never happen. I wanted a prayer take-back. I promptly said, "No, God, I was kidding. I am just requesting that I would really like my period soon." I tried to explain that I was the only one in my group of friends that hadn't yet received it. "Please help me out" and a simple thanks were the end of the appeal.

A year and a half went by and no period. This was a frustrating time as in addition to not having my period, I often felt that something in my life was absent. I just didn't feel present or connected. There was a void which is hard to put into words. I was often putting pressure on myself that I wasn't as smart as Julie. I also never felt completely at one with my form, even though I was blessed with Mum's great legs and Dad's family trait of some shapely lips. In my heart, I knew there was something I was missing. At highschool, I enjoyed English and biology, but I often cut other classes or I would arrive late, as most topics just didn't engage me. It was to my advantage that Julie had set a studious example at the same school three years earlier. The teachers, in the hope that I would be another prize student, would often cut me some slack. The art of negotiation was a natural ability of mine. I had some great one-liners on why I was late to class or why my homework was not done. Thanks to Julie's high performing track record, I seemed to get away with it.

This first year of highschool, our first poodle was put down after allegedly falling down the stairs and incurring substantial injury while I was away on camp. I heard how he couldn't walk and that the euthanasia decision had to be made then and there and could not have waited until I returned home. I was very close to this dog and felt absolutely devastated I wasn't there to say goodbye. My distrusting nature made me think he hadn't had a fall and that my parents considered it was prime time to end an aging dog's life so I wouldn't protest. Emotions were fraught with a mix of anger and sadness, and even hatred arose. "I will never forgive you!" I screamed when I found out what they had done, completely forgetting that the rest of my family was grieving too.

With time, those emotions settled down, or maybe I bottled them away. Then to my surprise, one weekend Mum announced we could go to the SPCA to look for a new pet. When we got to the shelter, we looked around and I saw this long-haired tabby cat. I instantly knew he belonged in the family. Julie and Dad spied this pure-white feline that flashed them with a "pick me" look. On the way home, my kitten had a toilet incident in the car and sat in it, making a mess everywhere. So aptly named Smudge, and newly titled Josh, had just joined the Maude clan. On my arrival home, I needed the lavatory myself. "Oh my God" quite literally. My excitement wasn't for the fact that I was now in the elusive group of ovulating women. It was the constant pondering on the amazing coincidence. How uncanny that I received my period on the unlikely day when we got cats, as per my request. I wondered what other wishes I would get granted from above. This absolutely amazed me for all of a few days and then my humanness took over and I forgot.

Old Man's Ears

Old man's ears
Are amazing to me.
I bet in his young days
They never used to be.

A jumbo-size flap
From his head so protruding,
How they keep growing
Is really deluding.

It now has been proven
Scientifically so.
The real reason why
Is what I want to know.

To amplify sound,
An evolved hearing aid.
Do I need to accept
That's just how man's made?

With wiry ear hairs,
An elongated rim,
Gravity-stretched lobe,
And sun damaged skin,

The owner of these ears
Is oblivious to this,
Smiling with knowledge
In his old-age bliss.

Chapter 3

The art of creation is the space where things just flow and you feel good about what you are doing. I have had many times in my life where this has been the case, and it's even better when humour is included. Dad had an awful habit of picking his nose and flicking it off his finger with no concern on where the offending bogey may land. So I decided to make for him one birthday a bogey keeper. Made from a cardboard cube cut-out, neatly folded into a lidded box for which he could store his nasal debris. On presenting the gift, he laughed and accepted the underlying message to keep his bogeys to himself. Throughout my life, I have dabbled in various crafts which included making jewellery and painting canvases. There were some cringe projects like hubcap clocks, wooden cat doorstops, and under-formed paintings which were given as gifts, but the love and passion that were put into each art piece was reflected in the giving. Some items were thought of as fashionable for the time and friends and acquaintances even requested them. When I started to mass-produce for cash, the buzz diminished and I generally moved on to something else.

The need to learn my nana's sewing skills never came to full fruition. Even though I often had half-hearted aspirations to whip up a piece of clothing on impulse, I was never really committed to investing the time to do things properly. My yearning to create persisted throughout the years. When knitting came back into vogue, advertised as a relaxing hobby, I decided to give it a solid attempt. "Calming and therapeutic" the ad stated. I don't think so! I found this the most stressful craft of them all. How can a simple scarf nearly turn into a blanket? I wasn't dropping stitches; I kept splitting the wool and gaining them. My fingers would grip the knitting needles so tightly like they were something to be conquered. My shoulders were raised and my muscles became tight. I was battling with my mind's relentless message of *Quit. Give up. It's awful.* There was no denying the fact that this scarf was not fit for purpose. This knitting project, like many sewing attempts, was shoved in a cupboard. It was looked at on occasion, with fleeting thoughts on whether it should be rectified or discarded. I had to admit knitting was not my forte; however, fashion co-ordination and home décor are flares I do enjoy. Cooking with fresh, balanced flavours is a skill that I wish to cultivate, if I could only gain the patience to follow a recipe properly.

In my adolescence, I was lucky enough to have the opportunity to learn the basic levels of music. Mum's instrument selection for me was the piano, as the recorder, my instrument of choice, wasn't the sound she desired to hear in practice every day. I had piano lessons for years, but the lack of appeal I had to the style of music I was being taught really disengaged me. I was always distracted when it was time to run through the exercises. Isolated in the dining room while the family was at the other end of the house watching television, I cunningly worked out ways of cheating at practice. The radio-cassette player with its built-in microphone came in handy. I would play a tune once for which I would record and then play it back various times to give my parents the perception of a long, enduring rehearsal session. This gave me time to escape into my world of thought and doodling. Mum wondered why I continually hit the same incorrect notes and contemplated why her hard-earned cash for the lessons never seemed to see any improvement in my skills. She realised I wasn't enjoying it, so when I asked to stop the lessons, she decided not to waste any more money and let me quit. This was upsetting for her as she had also given up piano lessons in her youth with considerable adult regret.

I did have something that I liked to do, which was to write little verses. I enjoyed putting together rhymes that would tell a miniature story and I loved the way some words sounded and matched coherently when in rhythm or rhyme. I also enjoyed seeing the smiles or tears when these works were being read internally by the recipient. It became a custom for me to write small poems in Mum's birthday and Mother's Day cards. If I ran out of time to get inspired to write a poem for her, I would get flashed with a childlike look of disappointment. I now try to keep up the challenge of applying diverse new themes for my written text in her cards. My aim is to expand our thoughts and to stir new feelings within us. To hopefully cultivate enlightened perceptions of this life we share together.

Some great ideas for creative initiatives would often come to me in daytime dreaming sessions. However, as soon as I got excited about them, my mind would take me on a path elsewhere. These blossoming thoughts would get lost in a sea of procrastination, never to be put into action. I would often block these revelations with mind-numbing events like watching movie reruns, getting something to eat which was not to satisfy physical hunger, or the need of some nutrition. No, I was just on the creative stalling train to complacency. In my late teens, drinking sweet bubbly wine was also an effective tool to get out of the chaos in my mind. I just couldn't work out why I felt continuously disengaged with life. I had most needs met with a great family, home, and friends, so why was I not content with my current life experiences? Nothing gave me the feelings of happiness and satisfaction I knew life could offer. I would see others with heated passion and drive to accomplish their dreams, yet I didn't seem to know what my purpose was. I couldn't get out of my head the internal discussions on how I wasn't really that good at anything. I continually berated myself with the undesirable thoughts of not being perfect. Was this just the developing hormones to feel so uncomfortable within myself? I didn't give myself the time to truly analyse the question, so I just continued to fuel the feelings of not being good enough. When I did have creative moments which gave me snippets of joy, they were so fleeting they didn't stay for long. I just couldn't seem to appreciate the small stuff that my senses and surroundings were offering me. Don't get me wrong. I could have a laugh and have fun, but in most enjoyable events, my mind would end on a negative comment to bring me down a notch. Was this to hold protection in place, to shield me from parts of this reality? In physical appearance, I had things in the right proportions. I had co-ordination for many sports, but I was never motivated enough to excel at any of them. I could study and get results when I wanted; however, my appetite for living life to its full potential was absent. Was I resigning myself to a life of being ordinary? I was constantly disappointed that I couldn't find that one thing that would engage my soul to achieve something great.

My detached presence to life left me feeling extremely flat with cravings for something I didn't know how to satisfy. My sister had a God-given gift of a beautiful singing voice which she trained into a heavenly operatic style. I was empty that I wasn't able to recognise what my gifts were. Yes, I could write little poems and make people giggle on occasion. *But anyone can do that*, my mind kept advising me. My ego wanted something grand to brag about, but in my heart, I yearned for something more.

My teenage years embraced New Zealand's culture for binge drinking. This escapism from uncomfortable feelings wasn't really recognised as such as drinking was deemed normal teenage behaviour, and it was fun. Street parties gathered great crowds and usually ended with us being ushered down the streets by the police, who were trying to disperse the intoxicated student masses. Smoking was also prevalent in my environment, having two parents that were truly hooked. This was before the real negatives were publicly acknowledged of this habit, so it was acceptable conduct in that time. I did try smoking, and luckily for me, this addiction never took hold. However, alcohol, and to some degree the sweet, pleasurable taste of sugar, became solid friends early.

I find it quite interesting how there was slight praise for being a bit naughty growing up. Reminiscent of the time, I pinched one of Dad's bottles of high-alcohol home brew beer to skull before a school social. After consumption, I dropped the empty bottle out of my bedroom window onto the soft ground below with the intent to collect and discard it early the next day. Morning panic set in when I was woken with the sound of a lawn mower, knowing full well an empty brew bottle was not what I wanted Dad to find while cutting the grass. Too late! The mild telling-off I received for pilfering a bottle of his lager was outweighed with the comments of how he was quite impressed that I knocked back the sediment which was always discarded and never consumed.

Home brewing for Dad was one of his creative activities that he loved, even though he was susceptible to our family trait of not having a drinking off button. I am not sure if this was genetic or just pleasure conditioning, as it stands to reason we always want more of what seemingly makes one feel good. Even though his hobby had an addictive capacity, there was joy in his eyes when he explained how he developed the unique flavours of each batch to his guests when entertaining. He was extremely proud of what he was making.

My parents' pottery business had the benefits of enabling them to be creative and follow an artistic passion for a time. They could nurture the development of their Cindy Ceramic range of cups, jugs, and flan dishes. Their brand was proudly displayed for sale in the nationally renowned Farmers Trading Company department store. It was very sad the day that imports became so cheap and small local businesses were pushed aside for mass-volume sales. So after the family pottery business had to be folded, Mum obtained an office job and they invested in a small hardware business to buy Dad a job. This business, purchased on the cheap, was located in a less desirable location of Auckland. Dad would keep a replica pistol under the counter to scare any shoplifters; however, over time he made friends with a few of the locals. The shop had a gardening section and as Dad had some green fingers, he enjoyed up-skilling in this area. In a moment filled with naughtiness, he accepted the offer of some marijuana plants from one of his regular customers. He took the plants home and cultivated them into sizeable budding bushes. As I was starting to mature in my late teens, my parents seemed to have a need to act out with middle-age mischief.

My seemingly straight-laced parents were rebelling against the rules. On a weekend away, they took some herb with them and then felt the need to call me to ask how to keep their joint alight. The laughter I could hear in the background of the phone conversation wasn't from the brain chemical alterations from smoking. I was pretty sure it was due to the fact that they were free from responsibility for a change. Mum's principles did set back in when they got home. As she felt they were not setting a good example, Dad was ordered to get rid of his fine specimens. Let's just say I stayed around for the bonfire that day.

A gardener's green fingers, an artist's hands, or a poet's mind all invoke creative energies to flow through them. I'm sure there's something quite surprising within all of us just waiting to be uncovered. I'm trying to develop the art of being composed at the moment when these forceful energies arise, so I can cultivate them into their intended beauty and purpose.

Andrea Louise Design

I love to create,
Inventor or not.
For my dad I made
A box for his snot.

Oh yes, I recall
As a proud young thing,
The card cube was made
To put picked bogeys in.

I am pleased to say
My skills have progressed.
With colour to canvas,
I dream out my best.

My stories of words
From visions that thrive,
Born with this joy,
It gives me life's drive.

I move into flavours
A culinary flare.
The scientific balance,
One day I'll be there.

Passions give purpose.
Here's a challenge to do:
Be still for a moment
To find what's for you.

Chapter 4

In my midteens, I started regularly seeing 11:11 on digital clocks, and the occurrence of this was too regular to be a coincidence. I felt like it was a signal to something, but at that time, I kept thinking it indicated a warning of some kind so I became fearful of it. My lack of understanding made me try hard to dismiss my sightings of it. Mum saw an article in one of her women's magazines about another lady who kept seeing the same time prompts. She too had the same burning question I had. "Where is this coming from?" Over the next ten years, its prevalence for me would come and go.

On leaving school, I was unsure of what I wanted to do with my life. I didn't enjoy intense study, so there was no real calling to attend university. Another year of learning I could handle, so I enrolled in a veterinary nursing course due to my love and connection to animals. There was a lot of information crammed into this inaugural course, yet the lecturers were upbeat and energetic. My quiet demeanour in class didn't make me stand out to be one of their highly potential nurses. I was continually distracted by my dissatisfaction in life. One female tutor was so high on life she incessantly kept verbalizing, "No matter how old you are, just keep learning." When that statement was made, I instantly thought, *What is the point? We die and it's all gone.* Nevertheless, I decided I couldn't fail and waste the tuition money, so I put some long hours into revision for the first exam. The educators were shocked at the 98 per cent accuracy I managed to achieve. This top-of-the-class result from one of their less inspired students definitely took them by surprise.

After I had completed my study, I managed to find a job in a vet clinic near the polytechnic, which was also close to Dad's shop. As poverty was still very prevalent in this area, clients would often get their animals treated, leaving semi-valuable or possibly stolen items to pay for their pet care. It was not an ideal working environment, so within a short time frame, I scoped out an alternative position closer to home, in a vet clinic on the North Shore. I witnessed, from working in the two very different clinics, that the wealthy and the underprivileged would do absolutely anything for their pets to relieve pain and distress, and I rapidly learnt the value of compassion.

In my vet nursing role, my responsibilities included the management of the clinic when the vet was out on house calls. Flea treatment applications, pet nutrition advice, and unfortunately, cleaning were all part of the job. The dental work and surgical experience gained in my employment were interesting; however, I knew becoming a vet was not my vocation. Four years on, I was getting bored, so when my boyfriend at the time was offered a job in Tauranga, a developing town three hours south of Auckland, I leapt at the chance for change. This relocation, however, didn't give me any instant clues on what my true life desires were. I ended up taking a job selling insurance, and to keep a connection with the animal care industry, I also accepted a Saturday position nursing. Things were going reasonably well and a brand-new home was purchased, which was a great start in my early twenties.

The years progressed with the standard milestones that we often seem to measure. My partner was self-employed with a weather-dependent trade, so when money was tight, my stable income was critical. This is why panic set in when an extensive corporate restructure was announced for the insurance company I was working for. Relief quickly followed when I was one of the few staff members who managed to stay employed. Tauranga was a small, developing town which wasn't quite growing at the employment rate to take an influx of over forty unemployed people at once, and for many, it became quite a tough time. I was so relieved I had secured a job with three others in the smaller sales centre, and the upside for me was that these people became my very close friends.

Two years later though, I needed another change and the timing was impeccable when I saw an advertisement in the paper for a pet food sales representative. The role was with a renowned privately own company and the position was Tauranga based. These opportunities didn't come up often, so I enlisted some help from my sister, who was skilful at embellishing past achievement to make a great résumé. I obtained an appointment to meet with my potential new employer. I was terrified at the prospect of the interview. The advertisement indicated candidates would be expected to complete a formal presentation to their leadership team on an allocated topic, which would only be given on the day. Various personality and mathematical tests would also be part of the application criteria. I had to gather up all of my mental strength to push me into this challenge. Just thinking about presenting on an undisclosed topic made me so nervous that I kept profusely sweating. I knew it wasn't going to be a good look to have massive sweat marks on my business shirt when presenting to a boardroom full of people, for which I was trying to impress. Instead of bailing on the interview, a friend at the time was breastfeeding her first baby and we thought out a solution to use breastfeeding pads as sweat collectors under my top.

On arrival to their office, I was welcomed and advised I had forty-five minutes to prepare a hypothetical business case for a relaunch of a chocolate bar. This was also a confectionary company, so I had to get my head in the wider business game. I mapped out my fictitious strategy and I was successful at the role-play presentation. All seemed to go well; the breastfeeding pads had done their job. Once I was out of the building though, I attempted to find them in my undergarments, which I had used to secure them in place, but they were gone. The nauseous feeling that came over me when they were not under my armpits was horrific. I had a haunting visual of them lying on the boardroom floor which one of the business managers would have to pick up. My body was so affected by these thoughts I nearly vomited, then to my relief I found them at my elbows. I must have made an impression though, as the following week, I was invited back for another interview. And in no time at all, I was offered the position.

I had just secured a massive salary increase, a new car to drive around in, and the freedom to implement new business in the animal health retail sector. This exciting new adventure was just what I needed. This corporation was in rapid expansion and money was being invested for significant growth. Business conferences were organised with no expense spared and I attended some lavish parties, the likes of which I had never been exposed to before. Helicoptered to hills in Queenstown for morning tai chi to recover from the unlimited cocktails consumed the night before was a little excessive, but I was lapping it up. I was at an age that I could party all night. I was relishing this ride, but my bubble soon burst with a major falling out with my partner. Then my much-loved Nana Oli passed away. Why did joy always seem so short-lived?

These events became a catalyst for some decisions to be made; with my relationship over, I needed an escape. Julie and I had received an inheritance from Nana and we wanted to invest the money in something memorable, so it seemed perfect timing to do an excursion around Europe and a few other countries. When it was time to go on the trip, I had reunited with my partner. However, I still felt the calling to go and explore some of the world to see if that would help me gain some insights into what my life was lacking. Nicole, an old school friend of mine who was also living in Tauranga, decided to run away from her current relationship debacles and joined our adventure. So three excited kiwi girls set forth to see some of our world.

We had a relaxing time sailing parts of the Turkish coast one week, then partied hard while on our chartered bus trip. We saw amazing contrasts between idyllic townships full of love and worship and unpleasant places rife with human and animal abuse. My gratitude for my life in beautiful New Zealand definitely increased. On my travels, I had a lot of time to think and established that I still didn't really know the real me. I had a longing for something more, but more of what?

On my return home, my partner proposed marriage, for which I said yes. Now that I look back there was some hesitation with my answer, but we had been together for what seemed like forever, so I couldn't visualise any other life.

A few years later, we had a fairy-tale wedding. The day was amazing with everything going to plan thanks to my perfectionist preparation, yet only ten months later, the marriage was over. I certainly didn't see that coming. Together for eight years and married for ten months, what a disaster! I reflect on it now with appreciation as another one of life's tutorials, although at the time, my whole world was turned upside down. I had a job that was meant to be based in Tauranga, but I longed to be at home in Auckland with family.

After a while, I managed to obtain an Auckland-based role in the food-service sales team within the same company. This kept me from dwelling, on my now unmapped future.

My 11:11 time prompts became prevalent again. It felt like I was being monitored and I needed to find out more. The Internet wasn't active then, so I had to search for further information on this phenomenon. I combed many bookshops until one day I found a reference, a book called *The Journey into the Spirit World*. I read this book of someone else's experience seeing the same signs from spirit, yet I still wasn't sure what this meant for me. I wasn't even sure if I really wanted to know, as the unknown was a bit scary. Over the next few years settling into my early thirties, I was enjoying living with Julie, as she had kindly relinquished her flatmates to let me live with her. I dated a couple of guys over this time, but nothing lasted over a year. Nonetheless, they taught me various values, some that I chose to add to my collection and some that I was absolutely positive they could keep. I was ready to find love again and knew I just had to open myself up to the possibility that I was going to find someone that had similar principles to me.

Announcement: "The frivolous spending has to stop!" The food company I was working for needed to start making a real profit and costs were being cut from all areas of the business. Staffing restructures became an epidemic and it was "out with the old," with not so much of "in with the new." Direction got lost in the changes, to say the least, and it was very exhausting. Employees were very disconnected from each other. The majority of staff felt the need to protect their own turf. It was a shame I was never offered redundancy, as I desperately wanted to move on. A previous manager of mine knew I was in the job market and enticed me to another massive food company with a considerable packaging increase. But this corporation was not short of its own challenges. Talk about jumping out of one flame and into another company fire, but it was a great learning process to assist me in moving up the corporate ladder.

The new work social scene was in full swing. Wining and dining became common practice, yet I continued to desire a romantic companion to share my life with. One corporate event, a colleague and I were somehow seated for dinner with the chief financial officer of the global business, which did have its perks, as some premium wine was flowing. As the night moved on, inhibitions were lowered and relationship conversations started. My co-worker thought I would get on well with his flatmate Kevin, who was also a bit of a wine lush. I gathered some courage the next day and arranged a dinner date with him.

Things moved quickly and we would have been living together within the first month, if it wasn't for me sending him home one night a week so he wasn't officially cohabitating with me. I had developed trust issues which I still needed to work on, but I started to feel I had found my one. We both loved our free lifestyle, spending money on the nice things in life with no responsibilities. There was no real direction, but we were having fun. I was investing in the property market. One of the houses purchased was a joint-venture renovation with Julie. The plan was to convert, a massive home into two separate living areas. I had corporate sales junkets to Las Vegas and Fiji and I often wondered how I managed to secure all of this with no university degree or any real drive. Life seemed to be paving its way on its own.

In the back of my mind, I knew I was going to have a family at some stage, though my maternal yearning was weak at this point in time. Kevin, being eight years older than me, was similar in a way to Dad, who seemed content with letting things just be. I struggled to obtain that same relaxed style as the burning question remained: what was my true function in the world?

Another five years passed and it started happening again; the economy was changing and business costs had to be cut to give shareholders confidence in their investments. The business I was working in was slashing costs, mainly in the people stakes. This restructure was handled poorly so morale was very low. I just wanted to work for a company that had similar values to mine, and I didn't think that that was too much to ask for. On my first review of the Internet job site, a role instantly popped up with my name on it. Granddad must have been watching, as it was at the pink sugar refinery he liked so much. Once again, I felt like I was being looked out for from above and I was appointed as the food-service sales manager. I rapidly grew this sales channel and enjoyed the friendly and less threatening corporate environment. My career was moving forward, but in true form, it wasn't long before something had to throw me a curve ball or three to shake things up. My cat Utah, whom I had acquired in my vet-nursing days, died of liver disease. We also had to put Jake, the family poodle, down due to an old-age seizure, and not long after that, Dad got a cancer diagnosis. Why, why, why?

When Dad's days were coming to an end, I could tell he wanted to go. My family camped out in a hospice centre up north. This was the closest facility to Mum and Dad's beach bach, where they had set up for retirement. Dad was heavily medicated on morphine, but his personality would still appear now and then for us to have some level of conversation with him. One day I could see the life force energy in his eyes was all but gone. Mum was down the hall talking to one of the doctors when I had a feeling he was about to pass over. I asked Julie to play her own recorded music that she had put onto a CD for him. As her divine voice vibrated peace and harmony within the room, I said, "Quickly go and get Mum." Seeing Dad look at me just before he took his last gasp of air, I felt relief for him. The pain was ending and he could move on to his next adventure. I didn't really seem to be that upset; my mind kept giving me niggling remarks, making me feel uneasy that I was slightly devoid of the usual emotions that an event like this should trigger. I watched Mum and Julie grieve deeply as I pondered the thought on what was next in Dad's eternal plan.

Six months after Dad's passing, Julie was travelling with a friend in Vietnam when a typhoon hit. Mum and I were distraught, as we couldn't contact her for more than twenty-four hours and news reports were not positive. I think I cried more for her potential demise than I had for Dad's expected departure. Mum and I mourned together on the possibility of losing 50 per cent of our family within half a year. To our relief, we received a text message when communication lines were restored. Our tears certainly dried up when she informed us she had spent the entire event stuck in a bar, thigh high in water, drinking cocktails and singing with the locals. Our prayers for her safe return were certainly answered.

This event seemed to be a catalyst for Mum to live life to the full and move on to her next stage of life. As Dad's sickness had lingered for quite some time before his passing, Mum had already grieved heavily. So when a romantic interest came from one of their friends, who had lost his wife three years earlier to cancer, Mum found herself a new companion. She had to work hard to let go of the notion that people would judge her for getting into a relationship relatively soon after Dad's death. I feel Dad would be pleased that it was someone that he knew and cared for as a friend.

With Julie safely home, things became comfortable. Our poorly forecasted one-year house-renovation project had moved into its fourth year. Julie was living upstairs while Kevin and I resided downstairs. We knew that we would have to make some future decisions soon, and the time did eventually come to sell when Julie met a new partner. Kevin and I decided to move into a small rental property I had just down the road, which needed a bit of work. We made a pact not to let this one take four years to do up. It certainly wasn't our dream home. I was pleased it was no longer rented, as various tenants were quite problematic. Kevin and I mapped out what we needed to do to make it look like an ideal home for the first homebuyer. We flashed it up with new carpet, a coat of paint, and a nice new deck, and we knew once this house was sold we would have a decent deposit to invest in our dream home.

11:11 time prompts started, and yet again, I couldn't seem to get clarity on it. I knew there needed to be more to our lives than just working and drinking too much wine. One night, lying in bed, sensing some heartfelt desperation and feeling immensely sad, I asked who was giving me these signals. I quickly got flashed with a visual of a creature that was not of a human form. I said, "Very funny, mind." But I knew there was something more to that sighting, as my heart was racing and I actually felt some excitement. This was my first introduction to my spirit guide and I intuitively knew it was not my mind playing tricks. I questioned some more and established that his name was Zalu. I didn't know very much about meditation, but it seemed to come naturally when I wanted to make a connection with him. I never had another visual of him in that time, although when I needed to grow trust in our conversations, he would make me smile with only the left side of my upper lip. This reaction was defined enough that I knew I wasn't doing it. I could tell he was desperately trying to give me belief in the process without freaking me out. I didn't get too many answers then, but at least I had started to realise there was more to my current material circumstances than just chance. Unfortunately, patience for spiritual development was not one of my strong points. It's funny how quickly I forgot parts of our meditative conversations or halted even trying to gain more information when the busyness of life took over again.

With continually increasing financial income, Kevin and I became attached to our wine habit. I became more agitated that I was blocking my spiritual and creative potential with any task other than being still to gain some answers. Consuming wine and feel-good foods certainly made me worry less, seemingly filling my joy deficiency. This only lasted so long though, until the dark feelings of emptiness would appear again. I knew my guides had something to tell me, but there was something not quite connecting. Was this a pivotal point in my life path for change? I wasn't sure how this would all unfold, but I knew I just had to have faith.

Labyrinth of Love

Labyrinth of Love,
I'm prompted by time.
Twenty years passed
To explain it in rhyme.

Guided by friends
Not quite all-knowing,
With love on their side,
That's what they are showing.

I followed my shadow
For so many years,
Dismissing my cues
To let go of my fears.

I've dug deep to find
Some of my hidden gems,
Accompanied by light
For I know where it stems.

The love in my heart
Progresses my thoughts,
To archive the past,
A forgiveness of sorts.

Once this was done,
I found a release
Like a wave in motion,
Ensuing great peace.

To then forgive others
Who may not yet know,
I breathe in these words:
For it's time to let go.

We're all here together
To learn and to love.
Let's value each other
Taking lead from above.

Chapter 5

My life continued with an average level of satisfaction. Nothing really new was coming into play, until one weekend a friend convinced me to do a mini triathlon event for females. I thought this may give me something to focus on to break my discontented routine. Our preparation was limited, but the training plan managed to get a group of friends together for a few laughs.

When the event date was upon us, we all drove down to a small township four hours south of Auckland for our athletic adventure. A certain amount of preparation time had been invested for the running and biking components of the race. However, as I loathed swimming, procrastination was prevalent where training was concerned. It was a shoreline swim, which meant I could touch the bottom of the seabed, so I knew I could survive even if I pretended to swim with my feet on the sand. On event completion, I felt a sense of accomplishment even though there was no real ambition to win or break any time goals.

Not long after this, another friend roped me into a small duathlon, which excluded any form of swimming. Perfect! Six months following this, I was standing at a half-marathon start line nervously waiting for the start gun. The jubilation was hard to contain when this twenty-one-kilometre run was through, and with a runner's high, I announced a full marathon was next on the list. All of my friends instantly dismissed the idea, so I made a commitment to myself this harder challenge was the next quest I could get buzzed about.

I knew that it would take a lot of determination and preparation to complete an endurance run that was just over forty-two kilometres long. I found myself a proven training regime which consisted of short-burst training and some increasing distant runs. Withstanding half-marathon training runs before work proved to be the biggest challenge. Kevin became my key support person, keeping me hydrated on my long weekend training runs. I was feeling confident with the level of training I had achieved, but ten days before race day, my legs decided they were over it. My muscles became like concrete. I was in so much pain, but there was no way I was going to pull out after so much effort. I booked myself into a sports physiotherapist and pleaded for her to fix me so I could still participate. Deep-tissue massage and acupuncture became the treatment plan. The pain was extreme when she tried to release the tension in my calves, but nothing was going to stop me. I had a goal to complete the run in less than four hours. For a novice runner, this was a decent stretch target.

Arriving at the start location on race morning, the nerves kicked in when I saw the gathering mass of runners. I needed an emergency trip to the Porter Loo. Words of advice: this is not a place you ever want to go into on race day, but you do what you have to do. My body instinctively knew what was ahead, so it made itself lighter with a nervous release. Holding my breath as I quickly exited the cubicle, I looked up to see the ever-growing crowd.

I was running alone so decided I would try to get as near to the start line as possible. On scaling a small fence to get closer to the front of the pack, I lost my balance and nearly did myself an injury, but a fellow runner kindly prevented my fall. I didn't let that rattle me; *I can do this,* I kept telling myself.

The starting shot fired and we were off. My running music played loudly through my headphones, keeping me to my set rhythm so I didn't burn out too early.

The half-marathon mark was rapidly approaching; Julie and Mum were my motivational support team for this marker. I passed the halfway line feeling great. My training had paid off. I was then mentally preparing for what was next to come. Kevin and another friend had agreed to be my track crew for the second half of the run. I was feeling relatively fresh at the thirty-two kilometre point, though not long after this, my muscle strength started to wane. I knew if I stopped to walk there would be limited ability to start back up. I remembered in my training there was a suggestion to visualise oxygen going to the muscles that were giving me grief, but what does oxygen look like? I held in my visual field a fresh oxygenated mist that I mentally took into my thighs, and to my surprise, this did ease the discomfort. So mind over matter did work, to some degree. I wondered if this was enough to get me to the end. The encouragement from complete strangers on the sidelines also kept me going. I crossed the finish line in three hours, fifty-nine minutes, and thirty-six seconds, so with only twenty-four seconds to spare, I had accomplished my goal.

One marathon in this lifetime was enough for me, although I continued to run just to maintain fitness and a sporty physique. I also started to dabble in a few other sports like golf, tennis, and squash. I was having some fun with friends and life was smooth, although not that inspirational. This was until my friend Nicole, the same friend I travelled Europe with, called to see if I wanted to attend a spiritual workshop.

This workshop was run by a woman who had left the corporate world to follow her spiritual calling, to teach others how to connect to higher wisdom. Her voice could reach such elevated vibrational tones, which seemed to enable us to switch to the right frequency channel, to sense various spiritually driven sensations. In her guided meditation, my eyes kept profusely flickering. This absolutely fascinated me. When I tuned in, I became flooded with emotion and experienced an outpouring of tears, which actually felt good. Nicole and I learnt in this workshop how to use a pendulum, a tool used to enable divine energies to help us answer some of our questions. It took some practice, but once the signals were established, it did help me select my first crystal. It appeared that this clear quartz chose me, similar to how a new pet is often gained through strong magnetism.

Returning home that day, Kevin was interested enough to let me share my experience. On Nicole's arrival home, she was welcomed with a witch's hat and broom placed in the middle of her lounge by her teasing husband, not surprising from a sceptical English policeman.

Even with this experience, I continued to feel lost, so I decided to go to a counsellor to see why I couldn't seem to get happy. On the surface, I seemed to have it all. But I was holding this emotional torment that was brewing inside for which I didn't logically have a known cause for. The standard thought-feeling-action triangle was brought out to try to unravel some bottled up-hurts. I knew I had deep-seated emotions around not feeling good enough, but as a smart businesswoman, I still could not work out why control was not in my court. I knew I had free will to choose my path but definitely something had a strong hold over me. At every creative or positive turn I made, a block appeared to stop me in my tracks, my wholeness was shattered, and I didn't know how to find the pieces.

Heart Led

Running with mind,
Something to prove.
My eyes are shut,
Yet forward I still move.

On my conveyer path
The gears run smooth.
A dead end arrives;
I jolt into a groove.

Falling so deep,
Making me kneel,
Not knowing why,
It doesn't seem real.

Distract with a fix.
It's no big deal.
Discomfort is blocked,
Not willing to feel.

Continuing to numb
For ego to score.
My inner soul speaks.
I ignore once more.

My heart says no.
There's truth to explore.
The breaks are applied,
To search for my core.

Chapter 6

The small house Kevin and I had finished doing up was now on the market, and the first offer we received was twenty thousand dollars over expectation. The excitement brewed and we started to make a few offers ourselves on nicer homes in the area. But often our price submissions were moments too late or didn't meet the seller's price requirements. This led to great disappointment for us. We then started placing offers on homes that didn't really fit the prerequisite list that I always had in the back of my mind for our long-term abode. My requirements included a nice, quiet cul-de-sac street so our future children could play with the neighbours, underground power so the street would look clean and tidy, and a sunny living area with indoor-outdoor flow. A beach house was also on my list, but I knew full well that central North Shore house prices, close to the beach, were well outside of our spending. I needed to be realistic, but I kept it on my mental checklist anyway.

Unfortunately, the sale of our house fell through as the buyer had overcommitted financially. This setback was really hard to deal with, as we knew open homes had to start all over again. There was sporadic interest but no other firm agreement that came close to the first one. Disillusionment set in, but I needed to stay positive.

I continued to scroll through the property advertisements daily, knowing our future home was out there, somewhere. One day, I momentarily paused on an advertisement for a large home out in Orewa, a beachside community north of Auckland. It was fifty thousand dollars outside of our budget so I flicked past this notice and kept scanning. A few months past and we finally received a bid for our house that we were willing to except. It was a realistic price so holding out for more money just to be greedy wasn't going to do us any favours. We signed a contract and the pressure was now on to purchase again. House prices were projected to rise so we knew we had to buy in the same market.

A few weeks after our house sale was unconditional, the property in Orewa was advertised again with a substantial price reduction. Luckily for us, their previous sale had also fallen over. We phoned our estate agent and, even though it was not her listing, we asked her to assist us in tendering for it. Within thirty minutes, we had confirmed the deal on it. The negotiated price was three thousand dollars less than our planned price point. It was walking distance to the beach and at the end of a cul-de-sac, with a beautiful Pohutukawa tree planted in the roundabout. The whole property was fully landscaped with an established garden. Our new two-storey house was so warm and inviting. There were great little cubbyholes that were perfect for hide-and-seek for my future children, and I just knew life here was going to be good. Apparently, there were many people wanting to make offers after we had signed our purchase agreement, but this time, we had finally got in first.

After a few months living in our new home, it felt like it was just meant to be, so the past disappointments now felt like thank-you moments. While sipping sparkly wine in our new spa pool, I thought how lucky I was. I had secured this great house, found Kevin's love, and we both had careers that financed what we desired.

Little did I know what was about to transpire to shake me out of this blinkered lifestyle I was setting up.

Lillian Place

Tick, tick, tick.
The wish list near complete,
Sadness on past offers lost,
Joy in the new knowledge
That this was meant to be.

Tick, tick, tick.
The still and quiet cul-de-sac
Happily marked off the list,
With its regal Pohutukawa
Poised, ready to welcome us home.

Tick, tick, tick.
The growth our garden shares
Softly feeds our thoughts.
Her abundant blooms so bright
Nourish our hungry souls.

Tick, tick, tick.
The secret rooms are ripe for play,
Awaiting the high-pitched sounds
From small excited faces
Of children set to explore.

Tick, tick, tick.
The flowing patterns of light
Calmly flood our living.
We forever embrace her warmth
With love for the house now ours.

Chapter 7

Christmas Day 2011, my family was gathered for a lunch celebration at our beautiful new home. I was feeling really fit and healthy, my sense of humour was on form, and we were all having some enjoyable laughs. It was not until later in the afternoon when I was opening a beverage bottle in the kitchen that I felt pain in one of my fingers. I thought I had just pulled the joint out of place so I wasn't too concerned and carried on enjoying the day. A few days after the holidays, the pain progressed to other fingers, and then to my large toes. I freaked out as I had given myself an unprofessional diagnosis of gout. Nana had this condition which often had connotations with alcohol indulgence. Had my partying days caught up with me? I took myself off to my local doctor for tests; however, nothing indicated this was the cause of the discomfort I was experiencing.

Over the next month, more random symptoms surfaced. At the gym, I could no longer do any weight training as my strength seemed to have been wiped out. I kept waking with unexplained intense, nauseous hunger, and my vision would intermittently go very blurry during the day, even though my optometrist advised my contact lens script had not changed. The physical weakness was in every part of my body and I found it tough to even get up the internal stairs at home. My daily running was certainly over and I had no clue what was going on. Driving to work each day, I would look outside and everything seemed false. The trees stood like cardboard cut-outs, glued to one of those box models I recall making at school when I was as a child. There was uncontrolled crying for no reason at all, and everything seemed to make me feel sad. I found watching TV difficult as I just couldn't concentrate. I just preferred complete silence. Feeling completely drained of energy, I went to a holistic medical centre looking for some answers. "Stress," the doctor said, but I wasn't entirely convinced. My home life was pleasant, work was manageable, so other than maybe overdoing the running and wine indulgence and still clinging to my perfectionism, things were relatively OK. Some of my blood was taken for routine tests. I was sent home with some amino acid supplement therapy and advised to rest. I couldn't relax, as I needed to know why I couldn't even hold my arm above my head to blow-dry my hair. I would wake up in the wee hours most mornings triggered by an overwhelming appetite and abdominal palpitations; sadness was all pervading and the body pain wouldn't leave me. I had to keep searching to find out the cause.

At this time, I started to have more frequent meditative conversations with my spiritual guide Zalu. I sometimes doubted the things that I was hearing. So I asked for him to give me a sign. He would make me smile or I would get flashes of light in my mind's eye, which did increase my faith.

I started my Internet research on the physical symptoms I was experiencing and H.pylori, an intestinal bug, matched some of my ailments, so back to the doctor I went.

I arrived at the clinic a bit early for my appointment, so I decided to try and get my body moving with a light walk down the street. I didn't make it far with my pervading weakness, so I turned around and headed back. Entering the drive of the medical centre, I noticed a green wheelie rubbish bin parked outside. Stamped in white on the side of the bin were the numbers 11 11. I knew I would get some form of an answer for my declining condition this time. I looked skyward and said, "Thanks."

In my consultation, I convinced the doctor it wasn't just stress, so I demanded further tests be done for my H.pylori suspicion. Over the few days, waiting for my new test results, I was more often in tears than not. I didn't want to be like this, so I thought I might as well try the suggested home remedy for killing this intestinal bug, which was drinking the juice of a cabbage. It was as disgusting as it sounds! I also followed the recommendation to roll around on the floor once the cabbage juice was consumed to coat the lining of my stomach. I could tell complete desperation was in full swing when I start saying, "Die, bugs. Die." I was hoping the people living next door couldn't see that their new neighbour was losing the plot. I begged for higher powers to give me some answers. I channelled a message in that day's meditation that I would be given some news the next day. Sure enough, the following day I received a phone call from the medical centre with a new diagnosis: glandular fever. Not a bug at all but a virus. At least I had an answer, or so I thought.

I was nearly five months into these strange symptoms when I got a confirmation for glandular fever, or Epstein-Barr virus as it is also known. I thought, as the lab test indicated a past infection recovery should be imminent. On waking each morning, after intense, unpleasant dreaming, the pulsating abdominal energy would start up; my whole being was consumed by worry with this illness. I wasn't able to hold conversations for long, which doesn't quite work in a sales management career. I didn't want to be around people, and I was so weak I had to take some extended leave from work for a time. I was able to cover the essential tasks for the team from home. Higher-level delegation wasn't one of my strengths. My perfectionist nature made me hold on to tasks in order for it to be done correctly. I knew I had to let go and entrust the sales team with new projects. This did help everyone's development. So with work worries mostly alleviated, I tried to give myself time to rest. Yet with my sheer frustration of not obtaining full clarity on the cause of my symptoms, my time was allocated to continually scrolling the Internet and researching in books.

After eight months, I was diagnosed with chronic fatigue syndrome with fibromyalgia; the weakness and body nerve pain was everywhere. I was fully aware that many people never recovered from symptoms like these, so my determined search began to look for more answers. I did have a mild immune disorder from my teenage years. My platelet count was low with no known cause, so off to an immunologist I went for a full review, then a haematologist, then an endocrinologist. I had all sorts of toxicity and nutrient deficiency tests carried out. My digestion had nearly shut down, although I was always ravenously hungry. Accidently while trying to unblock my nose from crying, I found that a menthol sniffer eased the hunger, but only when it was in use. Kevin started looking at me sideways when I continually had two tampon-looking vapour sticks hanging out of my nose. The erratic crying, weakness, and body pain were all-consuming. Every day I asked God to give me direction and improved health and I amplified my conversations with my spirit guide. I knew I needed all the help I could get. Surprisingly, various forms of valuable information did seem to naturally come to me and I was being advised from above to write things down.

The look of illness had taken hold in my face, I had turned a terrible shade of yellow, and a vacant darkness filled my eyes. There was an intermittent internal clicking noise in my brain and my tongue was swollen and white with strange circles expanding on it. Drinking green-leaf juices eased the nerve pain occasionally but didn't stop the extreme desire for full sweet flavours and high-energy foods to fill the energy deficiency. It seemed like my physical machine was not getting the right codes to make it all function correctly. How could a virus that was meant to have passed cause all of this?

I had to look for deeper meaning, so I sort help from a spiritual healer. He could see that my emotional field was distorted—not something I didn't already know, as I had always been a worrier. I had a healing session and booked myself into a spiritual workshop to gain some knowledge. I didn't have any real understanding of energy fields and chakras, yet I instinctively felt there must be something to it and I wanted to learn more.

In the workshop, I was given instruction on how to perform a prayer manifestation on a new moon. I thought it was worth a shot, so I pencilled in the date for the next moon cycle in my calendar. On the day, I set up everything as advised. I placed in a glass bowl three candles, which were positioned in a triangle shape, in some shallow water. I also had a pen and some paper to write my wishes for full health. During this ritual, I was running on autopilot, as my cognitive function was low.

Before I knew it, I had dropped the white robe that I was wearing. So standing in my meditation room, completely naked, I wrote three requests. I recall my surprise once the ceremony was over that my chosen wishes were not what I thought I was going to ask for. My first request written was "Please assist me in doing God's will that he has for me and that I have agreed to do for him." Second request noted was "Please enable me to find my true self and heal my life wounds from the past." Third request was "Please enable me to find unconditional love and teach humanity how to find it." "Love you" was my signoff. I reflected on the fact that I had neglected to include my appeal, for the complete healing of my debilitating symptoms. It was like my higher self knew what I wanted to ask for, and I guess to some degree it was true. I always wanted to know what I was doing here.

I was gaining awareness on the benefits of an organic alkaline diet, as my body was way too acidic. Yet I couldn't digest too much bulk, so even vegetables seemed to give me a food hangover. Emotional clearing techniques helped me uncover some earlier life experiences, and muscle testing assisted me in selecting supplements that would help me heal. I was gaining so much information about the physical body which made me realised how much I didn't know about it. I would go to the library and ask the divine before entering, "Please guide me on what I need to learn."

One occasion, sitting on a bookshelf completely out of place was an emotional healing meditation CD twinset. I played it on a regular basis and it did help calm some of the disruptive thoughts I was having. Books on biology, spiritual transformation, changes in the ages in 2012, and basic chemistry were all highlighted to be read. It seemed like I was finally finding things that were interesting to me but feeling so weak, sad, and disconnected it was hard to take it all in. What was I meant to do with this newfound wisdom? I didn't have the concentration or memory capacity to store very much of it, but I kept following my spiritually guided advice to write some of it down. It was also suggested I learn the Lord's Prayer, which I thought was an interesting request.

A healing open day at a local spiritual centre gave me the starting blocks for learning a form of energy healing. This included their teachings of a white light visualisation technique, where you imagine and sense light coming in through the top of your head and flowing like liquid through your body. To start with I had issues keeping my mind on the process so sometimes I thought of it like the scanning effect of a photocopier working down my body. I also learnt a channelling practice, where the light energy is directed out of the hands, onto a particular energy point or part of the body that needs restoring. I used this daily, which did subdue some of the uncomfortable pulsating energies that seemed to be worse in the mornings.

It was suggested I see a particular healer that had a special gift of sensing issues in one's auric fields. On our first meeting, he took a very wide berth around me and wouldn't shake my hand. Not a great sign, I thought, but I assumed he was just protecting his energy fields. He proceeded to guide me into an extremely deep meditative state. He then requested that I ask my body to tell me what the trauma was that was affecting me so badly. I pondered how ridiculous this seemed, as I was sure I knew all of my significant life events. After about five minutes, I started to get a pulling sensation in the quad muscle in one of my legs. It was contracting and lifting up to my hip with no deliberate intent from me. I found this quite fascinating. I couldn't force it; I just had to wait patiently for any other movement or feeling that may help tell the story. I didn't gain much more than that on my first session. When I practiced this at home, both of my legs started to rise up with bent knees into my chest. In each session, I would go deeper and deeper and my body would move into a foetal position while I was lying on my back. My whole body would shudder and I could feel this immense fear. The healer asked me to think about what this was trying to show me. I didn't really want to know. When my lower lady bits began to pulsate, the tears flooded my eyes. I couldn't ignore the fact that it seemed like my body was trying to tell me that it had been affected by some form of sexual abuse. I had no recollection of anything other than one incident when I was around nine that involved an inappropriate kiss from an adult male. That was a terrifying event in itself, but this seemed different. I questioned my body further; on a correct answer, my body would shake and emotions would unfold. This strange experience revealed an ordeal when I was four with a relative. Even though I couldn't remember it, some visuals of the location came into my mind. I wasn't sure I wanted to relive the suspected event. My body wanted to release this locked away burden, so I diligently worked through the process of forgiveness. This took some time to heal, and the more I progressed on this healing journey, more things were coming to light.

It had been over twelve months with no improvement with my condition. I was still in pain and the nightmares were rife. Sometimes in these dreams, I was being hunted, and other times, I was the murderous offender. I kept waking in a terrified fight-or-flight state with my heart racing. I don't think I was getting any restorative sleep at all. The hunger was so powerful that I would eat jars of nut butter in the middle of the night, which I knew wouldn't digest well. Some foods, when mixed together, would ferment and make me very sick. The cravings were out of control. Ravenous for meat one day, other days all I wanted was anything that contained high fat. Most days it was the comforting energy filled carbohydrate that I desired. They seemed to calm the anxiety, but often after consumption, the heightened electrical currents ramped up around my body. Even with all of these extra calories, I started to rapidly lose a lot of weight.

Traditional Chinese medicine was the next therapy I investigated, and I certainly found a traditional one. The practitioner was an elderly man who didn't speak any English. Entering his clinic for the first time was captivating. There were wooden boxes, built from floor to ceiling, at the back of this room. They were full of herbs that were completely unknown to me. In my first appointment, he surveyed my tongue, checked pulses, and asked me a variety of questions via his daughter, who translated for him. The diagnosis was blocked chi with dampness and a yang deficiency. Surprisingly, some of these things had been detailed in the library books I had been guided to read, so it wasn't completely foreign. My liver, spleen, and stomach energy meridians had issues. I wasn't sure if this was contributing to my consciousness being up in the ethers, but it was advised I had to get my energy flowing down. I persevered with the prescribed herb brews and acupuncture for some time. Occasionally the acupuncture did relieve some of the weakness when an energy block was released, but I still wasn't getting the results I desired.

I was hurting everywhere and my mental and emotional fields were in a terrible state. I felt like I couldn't be a part of society. I was desperate to get better, so I spent the little energy I had to keep investigating. My family and friends were very concerned, and they too were all searching for things I could try. A friend pushed me to go and see a naturopath that could clear out built up pesticides in the body. Interestingly enough, one of the poisons noted is used in most flea treatments. My exposure would have been really high in my vet nursing days and I never once thought of protecting myself with gloves or a facemask. It also made me think how toxic it may have been to all of the animals I had treated. My physical system had become so sensitive to all chemicals. I was definitely weaker in the days when the council had been weed spraying. My make-up and body products also gave me reactions, and most of the foods I consumed gave me some form of irritation. Salt gave me tremendous headaches and a constricting feeling in my head. With preservatives and anything artificial, my body seemed to know it was not right. The circles on my tongue seemed to increase when I had eaten out. My frustration was increasing, as I still couldn't find out why this was all happening.

Things were getting even more bizarre. One night in bed when I had nearly drifted off to sleep, this awful sensation of heaviness was creeping up my lower legs. It felt like something was entering them. They became so heavy I was petrified, and out of sheer panic, I started reciting the recently learnt Lord's Prayer, but the dreadful sensation wasn't going away. The only other spiritual clearing statement I had was the line out of the old *Exorcist* movie: "The power of Christ compels you." I couldn't seem to say it verbally so I was screaming it in my head. After saying it for the third time, the struggle ceased. I had never experienced anything like it. I was desperate to tell someone, although it was so hard to explain. Was I being possessed? Once I gathered up some courage, I did mention it to one of the healers at the spiritual centre I had been visiting. He gave me some protection practices to perform on going to bed and he lent me some blessed stones to place in my room. I still wasn't sure if the strange experience was being caused by a negative entity, but I was hoping I would find out soon.

My longing to be closer to the spirit world enhanced. I had amazing light shows coming into my mind's eye just before going to sleep. They started like the night sky stars, seemingly so close and bright like I was part of space. I would cry and feel homesick for anywhere but here. "I want to go home," I stated, to God. I did start thinking I was losing it, as I just didn't feel like I belonged here. Even though I had great support, no one could explain why I felt the way I did. I confirmed to myself that I would never give up. I didn't want to take the prescribed antidepressants recommended by one of the specialists so I kept trialling as many natural therapies as I could find.

The next detox method I moved onto was colonics, and after the first treatment, I could clearly see I wasn't digesting food properly. The stirred-up toxins did make me feel very sick. While in the grips of hopelessness during a colonic session, I asked higher beings for more answers, and with closed eyes, I acquired a very clear vision of a woman. I couldn't see her face, as her head was covered with a thick fabric headpiece similar to a nun. She was holding a baby like she wanted to give it to me. "Please tell me what this means," I asked, but the visual disappeared. I had a chuckle to myself, realising that spirits were still trying to converse with me, even when I was getting the crap sucked out of me. How embarrassing, but I am sure they see it all.

In meditation, I was introduced to my two other spiritual helpers. I had gained a close team of three that were really trying to get me to listen to them. It was a constant struggle to tune in and trust the messages I was hearing. There were so many random bits of information that just didn't make sense. Yet the answers would often come together, days or weeks later. I was building faith, and I guess giving me all of the answers would ruin the challenge of it all.

My guides suggested that I should write a small collection of poems, keeping them in my style of verse that I enjoyed. It was requested that I give them to friends and family to share some of my newfound knowledge so far, even if they weren't fully understood. This creative process did help distract me from my physical and mental issues. I had been given a time frame to make them into small books to give out at Christmastime. The title of the book and structure were also given. I didn't want to fail in my first channelled task, so I went out and purchased a red, refillable notebook and started to write and draw the ideas behind the stories in rhyme.

I continued to try to calm the raging energies inside me that seemed to be taking over. It did surprise me that no one in the medical profession could tell me why these symptoms were still present. I had days when my eyes stung so badly that it felt like they had undergone laser surgery. At other times, my inner eardrums were so painful, which I couldn't explain why. My teeth would ache and the migraines were excruciating. When I mentioned to my doctors about pulsating energies in my upper abdomen or solar plexus, they would look at me blankly. I knew there had to be some spiritual connection to all of this, so I continued to ask for divine guidance.

Defence

The light seeps through
The stiff venetian seams,
Too late for my body clock
Currently on high alert.

The nauseous hunger
Starts on conscious state.
Time to battle
Or get in flight.

Alpha wave sounds
Calm the nerves;
The meditative pond
Removes the ripples.

Negative thoughts
Creep to the water's edge.
I float them downstream,
As I soon will be well.

Chapter 8

I had to ease myself back to work. On my return, I did have various emotional meltdowns and colleagues were very alarmed at how frail and yellow I looked. They could see I was battling. I isolated myself in my office most of the time, as I struggled to be around people. I just didn't seem present in time and it took all of my strength to get through each day. Leaving the office at night, I would often get to the privacy of my own car and then the unidentified emotions would pour out. The tears would just flow.

My mind continued in its relentless negative chatter and I couldn't seem to control the cravings of certain foods. When complete emptiness consumed my whole being, I would despairingly ask, "Why me? What is this all for, and when will it end?" Just when I thought I was not being heard, I started to get feathers placed in my path in the most random places. I recall walking into a practitioner's waiting room and a soft, white feather was just lying on the seat for which I was about to sit in. They then began showing up in various places at home. In very sad, overthinking moments, they even started to fall from the sky and just float slowly in front of my car windshield. They were suspended in my visual field long enough for me to get the message that all is OK. Bursting into tears, I knew my angels were with me, but why didn't they just make me feel better? I knew there was a bigger picture here and I wanted to know it all; however, it seemed I was learning things in a particular order for a reason.

The light visuals I was experiencing started to change. They became very fluid with vortex checker patterns with maze-like circles intermittently moving into view. Sometimes, I was guided to put my fingers on my eyes and I would hear the call to hold firm even though the pressure was sometimes very intense. It would often start with just pure darkness with a small glow of florescent yellow starting in four patches which would eventually evolve into a glowing yellow eye. In some of the very intense downloads, the yellow eye would turn into a deep-purple eye, and at other times, blue pin lights would come darting out at me. It was liquefied movement of shapes and lights, sometimes accompanied by a ringing sound in one ear. I would have to try to relax to get any clear message on what this was all about. *Healing* and *recoding* were the words I often heard.

Work continued to be a challenge, but I enjoyed still having some involvement with the sustainability team, for which I had been a part of prior to getting sick. With my changing views on the world, I kept up the challenge to keep driving the various working groups to continually look for better ways to do things. This was in regards to supporting our people and environment. We even set up a worm farm on site to assist staff café composting and we also helped employees think about how they could implement some changes at home. I decided to take some of my own advice and set up my own organic garden and vegetable-waste recycling. This was indeed needed, as my heightened senses could taste chemicals on nonorganic foods instantly and my body soon told me when I had consumed some. I was diligently reading all nutritional labelling on pre-packaged foods and realised how much artificial ingredients were in them. Being in the food industry, I was starting to see that consumers were requesting products to come back to nature, which did seem to drive corporate change. I then felt some degree of guilt in regards to selling volumes of sugar. It was getting some very negative press and I knew the level of attachment I had to the pleasure it gave me. I had to park that worry for a moment, as I knew things were evolving in a way that was well above my awareness.

I had an increasing desire to help our planet without really knowing how or where to start. I was still quite fragile physically, but when I had gained some energy, I helped out at a few local tree-planting sessions. I would also try to make positive changes where I could.

Alarming situations kept coming to me in my dream state. I remember seeing our world nearly coming to an end with an explosion. In this dream, I was trying to get everyone to pray; however, I felt a force trying to stop me. It was like a scene in an action movie with an immense struggling to overcome adversity. I had woken up before I had confirmation that everything was OK, but I'm convinced it was showing me that asking for divine involvement is helpful.

I had been desperately asking for help with the internal battle that was going on within my body, mind, and spirit. I was frantically trying to wave the white flag and give myself the inner peace I so desperately wanted, but I don't think I was fully aware of the reasons for the fight. All of the literature I had been reading indicated our whole universe was changing. It was helpful when TV shows like *The Cosmos* started. I knew with all of the natural disasters occurring worldwide, there was some sort of cleansing going on. I felt like I was in tidy-up mode myself and I questioned if Mother Earth was doing the same.

With my quest to seek more knowledge, I signed up to many websites that emailed me daily messages. Some of the emails were spiritually channelled lessons and some articles were from scientifically researched sources. Topics seemed to present themselves at just the right time, linking to themes that had been presented to me prior. The hot topic at this time was all about manifesting your dreams. I understood the concept that the divine can help manipulate things in the physical world on request, and I was trying to practise this daily. Cars would reverse out of parking spaces moments after I asked for one. I would visualise an article of clothing I wanted to purchase, giving a clear indication of what it looked like and what price I wanted to pay. Surprisingly, the item visualised was usually obtained within a week, if not the same day. I had to remember my requests and be grateful when they came into being, believing that it was more than just chance. The more detail and feeling I put into the request, the greater the results. I had to have no expectation for the delivery time frame, so I learnt to just let things be. If something was paramount for me to know, gain, or accomplish, I diligently asked for it and visualised it daily. I also knew that united requests and intentions seemed that much stronger. When a friend of mine was looking for love, I requested this for her. I made suggestions for her to also send out thought waves in regards to what she wanted and to work her own action plan towards finding it. Sure enough, someone that made her happy soon came her way.

I knew now what I wanted to do, and that was to work with spirit to help others wake up to the choices we all make each day. This is in regards to how we treat others, how we take care of our environment, and how we care for ourselves. Trying to find out how I was to do this over my lower mind's persistent distractions was not an easy feat. All I could do was pray for guidance.

Wasted

Who is it for when you litter?
Who is to blame for your waste?
Who is the one who buys too much?
Doing it all in haste.

Why do we allow these wrongs?
Why do we look away?
Why do we make excuses?
"Try harder" is all I can say.

What can you change for the future?
What can you do right now?
What can you fix forever?
It's time to find out how.

When will it all be too late?
When will sorry be too weak?
When will our race step up?
Only then we will get what we seek.

Chapter 9

The last year working through these difficult symptoms did have an upside: with my weakened system, I had no choice but to give up drinking wine. Kevin wasn't quite ready to give it up. I could see now from a different perspective how much we were actually consuming. I worried that my cravings for it would always be there and I was also concerned that Kevin would stay reliant on it. He did manage to quit smoking, so I didn't push him, and my guides asked me to have faith that he would stop drinking when the time was right for him. I wanted us to both heal our habitual attachments that seemed to take us away from facing ourselves. Kevin did choose a date to stop drinking and, true to his word, we both became non-drinkers.

Eighteen months from the start of my ailments, I managed to gain some symptom-free days, which were accompanied by some happiness. The strange thing was when I started feeling well, I quickly went back to my old ways of living. Filling my days up, rushing here and there, and I would forget all of my new learnings on the benefits of connecting with my divine. Meditation got pushed aside, which may be the reason why my moments of reprieve were very short-lived. I had more to learn and illness seemed to compel me to progress on my path.

I knew I was on some sort of spiritual discovery journey with a come-and-find-me type of game being played out. Kevin kindly agreed to help me on my search. I asked him to attend an advertised 11 11 oneness gathering with me, for which he cautiously agreed. It became apparent that many of the spiritual events I was being shown to attend were all located on Auckland's North Shore. My guiding team was certainly trying to make this a bit easier for me.

We arrived for the registration and were welcomed to be seated in a large hall. I didn't really know what to expect. There were a lot more people participating than I thought there would be. Had all of these people seen 11:11 time signals too? There were so many of us searching for spiritual guidance. Some of the ideas that were shared at this event were similar to the knowledge I had recently gained, but in general, this event was a little haphazard in organisation. I wasn't sure I had gained that much from it.

When it was coming to a close, an announcement was made that it was time for a group hug and dance, so Kevin and I promptly worked our discrete exit strategy. On leaving the hall, I overheard another couple that was also departing quickly, making the statement that they would need at least a bottle of wine before getting involved in something like a sober dance and sing-a-long. This would have been something I would have said a year and a half earlier. I wasn't up for dancing with strangers, but I felt like there was a purpose for me being there on that night.

A few months later while sleeping, I was rocked by another peculiar episode. I felt like all of a sudden there was a thunderstorm directly in the room. I could see bright flashes of light and I was shuddering internally like I was in an earthquake. A loud roaring noise, like a jet engine, started up just beside my right ear. I was riddled with fear and completely catatonic so couldn't yell for help. Thinking I was possibly psychically attacked again, I tried to recite the Lord's Prayer, but I couldn't even recall how it started. I was scared for my life. I could hear voices in the room, and the extreme shaking felt like it went on forever. When it finally stopped, I was distraught, my heart was racing, and I had no idea what had just happened.

A month after this strange occurrence, I woke without being able to move my body and I could see a being of light to the side of me. I couldn't work out what it wanted though. These incidents pushed me to keep investigating. I finally discovered that these shaking sensations and noises were sometimes experienced when our energetic body can separate from our physical body. I didn't even know I had an energetic body, let alone what it was for, but at least I had some reassurance I wasn't being possessed. It was the start of an out-of-body experience or astral projection of sorts. I couldn't recall if I had actually travelled anywhere, but my curiosity wanted me to try to pre-empt an out-of-body experience.

I found a phone application that played binaural beats, indicating it helped to alter brainwaves to make a projection easier. I had recently purchased some quality noise-cancelling headphones, so I was all set for meditating myself into deep relaxation. I would then wait for the vibrations; sometimes, the anticipation was too intense, which just kept me awake. A few occasions just before drifting off to sleep, I felt tugging sensation at my feet and the internal tremors would start. As it felt like someone was there, fear kept snapping me out of the transition. I was a newbie at this and knew I needed to learn from people with more experience. I bought some books that gave me various techniques on how to control the projection process. Exiting the physical to project to other vibrational realms was something I thought was just in fiction.

It started to excite me that maybe I would get some of my childhood questions answered about what happens after we die. I did wonder if I should be doing this in my weakened mental and physical state. As I was exposed to this automatically, I assumed I was meant to know, so my practice began. I would take myself into a peaceful, meditative state, letting my physical body fully relax and feel numb while my mind stayed awake. I had to try to remain calm when the exit symptoms arose.

Lying in bed one night, the sensations started. The internal shaking felt endless. I couldn't seem to project up like the books stated, so I thought I would try to get my energetic body to fall out of my physical body, rather than elevating out of it. I could tell it had worked when the tremors stopped and all was still.

I recall feeling pleased that I managed to drop out onto the floor, until I realised I couldn't move. I had read that the projectable body works on thought commands. For the life of me, I couldn't function and I was stuck within the floor. My vision was hazy, but I could see beings in the room who were trying to help me. I clearly heard one of them explaining to the others that I was new to this. I remember once I was vertical, I looked down at my leg, and as soon as I did this, I was jolted back in my body. My heart was pounding, but at least I could remember most of what had happened. I was pleased I had managed to project but disappointed I wasn't out for long enough to learn more. I tried a few more times, but I wasn't that successful. I decided to put practice on hold for a while, as I was still very weak and needed all the sleep I could get and trying to project often kept me awake. I continued to meditate daily, and further pieces of information did surface for my awareness.

In a guided past-life regression meditation, I was shown a picture of a valley. It was located at the base of some green rolling hills. A woman wearing nursing attire was standing just to the right of one of the numerous army tents that populated this gorge. I could see her sobbing into her hands and I felt she was extremely upset. A tall soldier, dressed in a formal uniform, was trying to comfort her, but she was pulling away from his consoling embrace. I could see a baby in a tent and it was wrapped in a blanket, but I knew it was dead. I started to cry and knew this experience definitely had some connection to me. I couldn't get any further details on what had just taken place and why the child had died. I intuitively knew this visual was something I needed to expand on. Over time, I did gain more details around what I was being shown; her name was Maria and it was a life I had experienced. She kept trying to show me the lost baby in various meditations and I could feel her pain, but she was so upset the lines of communication were limited.

It was confusing me that I was having all of these amazing spiritual experiences, but my health remained in a terrible state. I was still working with a few doctors, trying to find new cures for my problems, but my impaired neurological connections exacerbated this dark depression that was setting in. I was rebelling against all I had learnt in regards to clean eating. The mornings were the worst as the energies on waking made me search for food like I was a starving animal. Inflammation became rampant with anything I consumed puffing up my face and ankles. Even healthy organic foods would cause terrible swelling.

I paid for more advanced tests for my physical imbalances and an intestinal strep infection was found. My neurotransmitter tests showed they were all out of balance, which was no doubt contributing to my increased pain perception and gloomy mood. No one seemed to know a way to get this system into alignment without the long-term use of drugs. I also couldn't get anyone to appreciate the magnitude of these munchies I had with this chemical imbalance. I was always on the hunt for specific foods to make me feel better. I rapidly started putting on weight. This was fine to start with, as I had lost a lot in the previous phase, but I started to tip the scales the other way. I rapidly started to outgrow all of the clothes in my wardrobe. I developed a compulsion to consuming mass amounts of milk and sugar, which only made the constant inflammation worse, yet it had profound calming effects on the anxiety I was facing. I then found caffeinated beverages helped to block the inhibitory substances my body seemed to be overproducing. It instantly brought some of my personality back, enabling me to be social again. But the very short-lived chemical change gave me increased discomfort and puffiness. I battled with trying to feel normal by using caffeine, milk, and sugar, knowing full well that it would inflict me with further suffering. The compulsions won for nearly a year just so I could engage with the world.

The deep depression that was engulfing my mental space was very disturbing. In my waking hours, flashes of bloody faces, sewer rats, and some very unpleasant scenes came into my visual field. One day while doing the dishes, I was washing the kitchen knife and I saw the mini cleaver slash my wrist. It wasn't a physical action, but the visual was very strong. In the fear I might get committed to a mental health facility, I didn't tell anyone about these visions. Luckily, I was strong enough when these things were seen that I managed to let them flow past. At the time, I didn't understand why I had these visions. Were they a part of me wanting to be cleared, like my historical clean-up, or were they from a lower group consciousness? I didn't feel like they belonged to me, but they wanted to be released. That was for sure.

My rational determination was compelling me forward. Even with the infiltrating mind fog, I continued to search for more knowledge. Thankfully, one day, I found an answer that linked all of my symptoms and visions. Described as a Kundalini awakening or spiritual transformation, it was also known to many as ascension symptoms. My experiences mapped to the physical and spiritual changes documented. It was a real phenomenon, and right then, I felt less alone. The more I searched this topic, the more people had blogged their experience. One website detailed the biological aspects of Kundalini, and other sites detailed more information on the spiritual aspects. I was shocked that it had taken me this long to find this out. In the doctor's defence though, I didn't really explain the visions I was seeing, but I am not sure how they would have handled it if I had. I continued to battle through what I termed my own spiritual, physical restructure. Like the businesses I had worked for, it was my time to toss out the old and encourage the new. How much of the old did I need to throw out and how much longer would this take? I accepted that

I had been releasing some old aspects of myself through visions, dreams, and recall, but in spite of this, I wasn't sure what would come next.

Perplexing impulses then started coming into play. I would hastily put shoes on as soon as I got out of bed, as it was very uncomfortable to be in contact with the floor. My body and hands would automatically conduct strange movements. This disconnect from reality got worse. It was like part of me had left.

Oddly enough, I had recently read an article about some autistic children who also had milk addictions, gut imbalances with severe food intolerances, and neurological abnormalities. In quite a few cases, the kids would walk on tiptoes to not touch the ground. It was also written that many of these children didn't enjoying being around people. This was way too similar to what I was going through. As an adult, I had the benefit of some intellect so I could start piecing things together. In a spiritual sense, I questioned, "Has something pushed part of my consciousness out of me, or was this done with a divine purpose to gain more knowledge for our future progress?"

I managed to gain the confidence to tell Kevin and Mum about my findings on spiritual awakenings. I was excited to share all of the details I had discovered. Although I overlooked the fact that I had been shown this information over time and I could link it all together by experience. My family had no tangible reference point, so it became difficult for them to comprehend it all. Nonetheless, they lovingly listened to me with no judgement, just support, and they had absolute confidence I would get through it.

I decided I would drop the term *Kundalini awakening* into one of my medical consultations with one of my more open-minded medical practitioners. He did appreciate the aspects I described, but we both had no real solutions to how I could work through it. We talked about some Tibetan exercise he was doing for energy balancing and I also came across Kundalini yoga. I tried them both, but they were a bit too intense for the state I was in at that time. Breathing exercises and light healing did help, except the darker thought patterns persisted and the depression and fatigue wouldn't ease up.

My energy production systems were still not working and I disengaged even further from friends and from life. I still had to deal with a busy work environment, which was the hardest thing I had to withstand. Trying to converse with people was challenging when I just wanted to be hiding in a cave. I kept revisiting some of the international blogs other people had written about their upsetting unexplained weakness, pain, cravings, and digestive issues. There were many of us searching for compassion and understanding through all of this, and we all seemed so fraught with the lack of solutions. The absence of resolutions didn't stop me on my quest to help myself and others.

On a work trip to Australia, I was reading an energy-healing handbook on the plane and the gentleman sitting next to me noticed the title of the book. I just blurted out my physical diagnosis of chronic fatigue syndrome, as I wasn't quite open to explaining my spiritual diagnosis. He mentioned he had a relative who had the same diagnosis as a teenager and found that swimming cured him over time, which I assumed worked by releasing some energy blocks. I knew physical movement would help my energy to flow, so I forced myself to walk along the beach barefoot in an effort to connect, but I struggled relentlessly with it. I just didn't want to ground to Earth. Kevin would try to encourage me on walks and lovingly hold my hand while trying to get me to go a little farther each time, but I just wanted to go home. We even purchased some paddleboards to try to get me into nature, but I didn't have enough energy or will to paddle. I fell deeper and deeper into isolation. I kept my days inside the office and my nights closeted at home while I tried to process my anguish.

I started to realise how much love Kevin had for me. Watching me go through this spiritual awakening was tough. Some days he had more faith than I did. He was truly convinced all was going to be fine. The lack of societal awareness of this transformational process makes the understanding of a caring partner so important in keeping things together. The ancient text says it can be transcendence or psychosis, and a few times, I came closer to the latter. I knew in the future Kevin and I would enjoy Orewa beach exactly how I pictured our lives to be. At that moment, I knew I just had to keep working on bringing my past into the light.

Visible Love

Our hands fit neatly
As we imprint our sand,

Sharing completely
As we pause and stand.

Facing the east
To view the warm glory,

We smile in awe
To glow a new story.

We journey together
In loving connection,

Helping to learn
In peaceful reflection.

Opening our hearts
To light that shines bright,

Binding true love
To an infinite height.

I've found my one
In a man that is caring,

Walking our beach
In a life that we're sharing.

Chapter 10

During the later stages of my personal restructure, I pondered the connectedness of many things occurring in my life. Mum owned a rental property in Orewa, which was only five minutes up the hill from our home. She had moved into the house not long after I started to get sick. It was so handy to have her close when I was so physically weak.

Nicole, my friend I made at intermediate school, who also shared the part of my life in Tauranga and who ran away with me overseas in our twenties, was living very close too.

Our family beach house at Glinks Gully, a remote west coast location, was a place that most people had never heard of. Yet this was a beach Kevin often visited as a child, and he loved going back there with me.

Facebook even helped me on my journey. I was not an avid user of this social networking site. I was one of those members who still had a grey head for not uploading an individual photo. In spite of this, I would view posts on occasion and some useful connections developed from it. An old work colleague was one of my Facebook friends. There had been no personal contact in many years, yet one day, her Facebook page linked me to an 11 11 awakening group page. The day that happened, she seemed to have cleaned up her database and removed me from her friend's list. I was not offended about this, as I could see that this 11 11 site introduction was the purpose. I felt that all of these networks and subtle links started to give me acceptance of the woven path of life.

Little nudges from spirit sometimes went unnoticed by me so more signs were presented until a message was illuminated. Other time signals became prevalent like 9:11 and 3:33. These were often sighted at the right time for me to take action on something. A prime example of this was their prods for me to learn reiki. A friend had been nagging me to train in this particular form of energy healing for some time. I just wanted to keep doing the other healing methods I had learnt, which on some level was helping me. I didn't want to put too much pressure on myself to learn something different. Then an aunt of mine, Dad's sister, came to visit from Australia. I really enjoyed her company, and her mannerisms reminded me of Dad. We got chatting one night on our health issues and she told me that her back pain was healed when she received some hands-on reiki healing from a friend. She was so taken with the profound effect this had on her that she completed a reiki course herself. Reiki information started coming to me from a few other sources, accompanied by encouraging time prompts. I then developed a sense of urgency to do it.

The tutor's home near Takapuna beach was beautiful and her training room was so peaceful. She attuned me to access the reiki healing energies. As soon as this was done, I could feel the force constantly flowing from my palms. This was so much more than the other healing methods I had learnt. The energy gates had been opened and it was astounding the amount of power coming out of them. I often had to put my hands on my body to relieve the pressure sensation of the energies surges. To my benefit, these energies were very quick at relieving my joint pain. I continued to use reiki on myself most days to ease the discomfort and I was enjoying offering this to others. Sadly though, my mental and emotional disruption wasn't yet corrected. I was not in the true sense suicidal, but I really didn't want to be here.

I kept trying to gain more understanding on Kundalini awakenings. There was a website that I was guided to which detailed information about Kundalini Starseeds. The picture shown on the opening page of this site made me cry uncontrollably. It was showing an illustrated picture of a dimensional being that looked just like the fleeting visual I had of my spiritual guide, Zalu. The site referenced that Starseeds were beings who originally incarnated on another dimension but could also journey to Earth. They could choose to take embodiment on Earth to assist the vibrational change process. This was noted to be more prevalent in the adjusting time we are currently in. What did this mean? Had I really started my soul journey elsewhere in an alternative form? My incarnational amnesia was starting to lift, but the magnitude of this discovery seemed like fantasy, yet in my heart, it felt true. What had I been taught about my origin anyway? Absolutely nothing! No one could ever tell me where I initially came from. The emotional impact of this discovery was so profound I couldn't doubt it, but again, who was I to share this with?

Was my situation part of the whole collective shift, moving into a time where it's said to be less separation and more unity? Was I mopping up some negative vibrational debris? Some of the visuals and dreams that I was experiencing were certainly trying to tell me something. I continually kept jumping from spiritual to physical symptomology, constantly looking for more and more reasons for why I was stuck in pain, depression, and compulsions. I was aware that some genetic distortions can be present in one's energy fields. I was hoping all of the work I was putting into healing my trapped emotions and self-imposed limitations would prevent my future children battling some of these issues.

I continued to be locked into this destructive melancholy. Then, just at the right time, I received an email for a healing night. The address was only a few minutes' drive up the road from work. I had no idea how I had been put on this list to receive this email, but I knew I had to go. Turning up to a stranger's house took some courage, yet I accepted that my guides knew what they were doing.

The main healer of this spiritually driven group channelled light language and healing templates for attendees to shift old lower vibrational patterns. Helping us all align with the new age systems that were being integrated. On the first night, the energies were so strong and being so sensitive I came away with a massive headache. I wasn't deterred and started attending each monthly session, gaining more and more knowledge for my healing. I thought I was the only spiritual apprentice there until I soon realised most of us had only just started to uncover ourselves. I wasn't aware then how much this group would become my spiritual family, and I soon realised that it was the 11 11 oneness event that put me on the original invitation list.

Earth's adjustments were opening us up to increased spiritual support. Energy vortexes were helping to bring in some changing frequencies and I was starting to realise my role in this changing time. No matter how bad I felt, I had a job to do. I was given so many indications to write. In a 2012 automatic writing meditation, I scribed that I was to write a non-fiction book in 2014. Unaware at that time what I could possibly fill a book with, I kept it in the background of my mind and continued to ask.

The spiritual group I was now a key part of planned a trip to Te Manaroa Springs in the Waikite Valley, for a magnetic energy experience. The travelling group was a diverse bunch of people, which included a modern-day Native American shaman, various healers, and light workers. It then dawned on me that I was one of those healing light workers. I was finally finding my gift. I longed to heal people, even though I wasn't completely healed myself. Was this like the builder that doesn't finish his own home or a mentor that doesn't take his own advice? I was working on my own healing constantly, so I had to give myself some credit. For this transformative trip to the Redwood Forest and Te Manaroa Springs, I offered to drive three other ladies to our destination.

During our road trip, we all shared parts of our personal journey that had joined us together for this excursion. Unfortunately, I was quite vacant on the trip, but I could feel the intense energies trying to help me shift. My light downloads started bringing in more geometrical shapes. Five-pointed stars were very prominent and the whole light administration became more intense. This trip invoked laughter and tears as more healing occurred.

The Native American shaman I meet on this trip became my next teacher. One of the workshops I attended was to learn about my soul purpose in this life. The message that was revealed for me was about learning and teaching self-worth. I attended a few other classes, but the most beneficial of the workshops was a soul retrieval session. The shaman conducted a retrieval ceremony to help me gather parts of my separated soul. I was seated in the centre of the group and was asked to think of some events that I thought may be affecting me. The shaman started the ceremony with some white sage smudging, which is the burning of this herb. He fanned the smoke while chanting and drumming in a circle around me. The scene was set for me to go deep to find and heal some personal traumas. I verbalised three events, the blocked child abuse issue that still seemed real even though I couldn't be sure it happened. I was asked to visualise the damaged part of my soul as a glowing ball in the incident location. I could clearly see a glowing ball of light under this bench and I was advised to reach out and put the piece of my lost soul back into my heart. I was crying so much as I worked through the experience. The next piece of soul to be retrieved was from the unpleasant incident when one of my parents' friends came into the guest room that I was put down to sleep in as a child. The feeling of fear escalated as I recalled him forcing his tongue down my throat. The shaman guided me again to find that part of my soul. I could see the glowing soul fragment in the corner of the ceiling and I brought it back home, releasing a vast amount of emotion. Then it came time to reveal what had happened to my child in my life as Maria.

The sadness was uncontrollable. As my crying increased, I could feel the whole group was crying with me. I couldn't work out the reason for the death and the guilt I felt. The shaman could see that a stray bullet had caused the death of my child. As soon as that was revealed, I visualised the scene where my husband had buried our child. I could see a large part of my soul up in a tree, close to the burial site. I put my hands out for its retrieval. I offered forgiveness to myself and Mother Earth for this loss.

The tears continued to flow for some time, and then an immense sense of calm filled my heart.

Healing my soul was only part of the task list. My physical condition still needed a lot of support in this change. I started to work with another acupuncturist who was also part of our spiritual group. She had strong intuitive abilities which helped direct her treatment plan. I guess to some degree I had been following my own intuitive direction over the last two and a half years. I had been guided in roundabout ways on which supplements would help in particular times of the adjustments.

The transformational information I had gathered mentioned that strong food cravings were amplified in Kundalini energy shifts, and mine were still present. However, some people remarked about having no desire for food. Yet most people indicated constant cravings, especially for carbohydrates. This was considered to fuel the transforming energies. Others expressed that the cravings were driven by emotions as a way to numb the difficult feelings that keep coming to the surface. I felt this could be true on some level as I did use certain foods to calm the uncomfortable. I did acknowledge that I had some extreme nutritional deficiencies, which exacerbated my unconscious consumption. This seemingly was to get the nutrient required, no matter how much the other ingredients would affect me. My new, higher-grade supplements did start helping with this though.

My body seemed to be lagging a bit behind in this vibration shift and it didn't seem to recognise most edible ingredients. My immune and nervous systems were extremely sensitive, so I was overreacting to everything I consumed. I had previously learnt that the sacral chakra energy centre did have connections with emotions, which could create attachment issues. If not open and flowing could also block joy and a zest for life. The solar plexus centre was noted to have links to digestion and self-acceptance. Reiki started to help rebalance this for me. I would place my hands on my lower abdomen and invite the healing energies in. Heat would come flooding through, and it would bring me some level of peace. Knowing that many of my issues were associated with my lower energy centres, I knew I needed to connect to Earth's grounding energies. There was still something in me reluctant to do this, so I purchased some silver-threaded earthing bed sheets to sleep on, to force myself to adapt. I also started listening to a reiki meditation download. The affirmations and frequency mix helped connect the physical and spiritual parts of myself. However, some negative aspects of my current mind still thought they had the right to maintain control. I just had to work out how to correct this, once and for all.

I could feel my permanent change was very close as I felt another phase of the shift. I started to get sensations that felt like running water over parts of my head and face. I would often automatically go to wipe it off, even though there was no liquid there. It was a light, moving, energetic sensation that I started to enjoy, as I knew it was restorative. About a week later, some of the inflammation started easing and the depressive cloud was beginning to lift. The nerve pain that I had been experiencing in my connective tissue was also dissipating. This was another level of the healing process and I was getting clear messages that I would be better relatively soon.

Kevin and I started to have conversations about starting a family; we had been thinking about this prior to me getting sick, but it had been taken off the agenda for me to get better. I had just turned thirty-nine so my biological clock was ticking. Going through all of this, I now had a completely different concept of what it meant to have a child. I wanted to give another soul a chance to heal and grow with, hopefully, the added bonus of helping humanity. I invited an enlightened individual to join us in this journey and started to feel the presence of an energy sussing me out. I was delighted I had found another life purpose. I started to look forward to the chance to offer encouragement and love to a growing human being.

I began to share my newfound skills with my work family, giving free reiki healings at lunchtime to many colleagues. There was a lady who was recovering from cancer who loved the feeling of the healing energies. There were others who wanted to experience reiki's stress and pain relieving effects too. I started to leave my portable treatment bed in my office, which prompted questions and more requests for healing. During a few reiki sessions, guided advice would come through, which I would subtly communicate to the recipient if it felt right. I was hoping these little pieces of information might spark something for their own spiritual progression.

I didn't intend to be working in the corporate food game for much longer. I had new passions to follow; however, I felt I had to be there a bit longer to help heal and bring a little more awareness in our changing time. I was happy that I could give small reminders to others to follow their intuition.

I was also grateful that throughout my awakening, I maintained a loving connection to my immediate relatives. Even though Julie had been living in Melbourne through this period, she still supported me in every step and had empathy for what I had been enduring. Mum persistently kept trying to bring me back to this reality when I was very disconnected. I also had some brief connections with Dad on the other side, which was so nice. I wanted to start sharing more of this experience with the whole human family. As many more of us start to release our past and expand for a more positive future, I hope stories like this will ease the ride.

Family

Applauding myself
For choosing my three,
My linking structure
On the branch of our tree.

My memories of Dad
Are of quiet support.
With steady presence,
His love never went short.

Mum is my food
For emotions to grow,
Expanding life rings
From the seed that did sow.

Big sister time
Our friendship profound,
Vibrating great warmth
With her heavenly sound.

From roots that are deep,
Family keeps weaving.
Growth in my vine
I just keep believing.

Chapter 11

As I progressed with my reiki training, I started to channel stronger healing forces. These powerful energies continued to help me unify my left and right, my masculine and feminine, my light and dark, and my spiritual and physical. The more I used reiki, the stronger it became. The beauty of this gift is that it is open for anyone to learn.

I also managed to find a naturally derived plant supplement called caralluma, that really helped ease the intense hunger I had been experiencing. Even though the dramatic energy changes were tapering off in this later stage, self-hypnosis managed to balance things even further, reducing the levels of inflammation and anxiety. This was just another form of meditation, adding specific suggestions to my subconscious mind. It was simple to do with current technology. I recorded on my smart phone a nice relaxation narrative to move me into a deep, relaxed state.

I would generally start my recordings by advising myself to take three deep breaths, following my breath through my nose, holding slightly on the in-breath and following the flow, in and out. I had to aim for low alpha or theta brainwaves so the suggestions would tap into the subconscious part of my mind. To enable that to happen, it was all about enabling my body to fully relax and narrowing my minds focus. I would take my attention down to my feet, letting them relax and get heavy. Then working up my body, directing concentration to one body part at a time, stating these muscles were getting nice and relaxed. Using words like *relax, deeper,* and *let go* made my whole body sink down into a type of slumber. Sometimes, I would make a suggestion to feel as if my eyes were turning over to look at the back of my head; this seemed to give me a level of detachment, taking me deeper.

Next, I would guide myself to look through my forehead, like I was looking out into deep space. I had been naturally exposed to this when I was receiving automatic divine connection, so it made sense that it helped when settling the mind. The personal dialogue recorded would depend on what symptoms were present at the time. Often, I would talk myself through visualising a peaceful scene, where I would see myself in a healthy, active way. Having fun, playing on the beach with Kevin and our future children. These viewed experiences had to have details on exactly how I wanted my life to be, or even just how I wanted the current day to play out. I had to feel the joy. Other times, I would give suggestions to bring in healing white light through the top of my head into every cell and organ, directing more into the areas that were affected by pain or inflammation. Then stating, "All is calm and well," and calling for the immune response to stabilize. I also visualised dual light streams coming down through my body, all the way into Earth, with a returning stream coming up from the centre of Earth, through my body, and out of my crown. All of these recordings were only about five to ten minutes long, which made it so easy to add to my day. Listening to them frequently helped to recode my subconscious beliefs. This also started to change the neural connections in my brain's reward and fear centres. At the end of each recording, I would count myself up from one to five, telling myself I was now wide-awake and refreshed. This made quite dramatic changes when a personal approach was taken. There were also so many specific hypnotic recordings available from the Internet for download, so if I couldn't come up with the right words, I had other options that were obtainable. Knowing that I had the power to reprogram my mind was amazing.

As my mind was getting into its new way of being, I was interested to learn more about the yoga positions and hand mudras that my body would spontaneously move into. With no knowledge in this area, it was incredible to find out that the life force energy was naturally trying move to specific regions of my body. What an incredible piece of equipment I have, which has just been nicely refurbished. I am learning to accept and love my human apparatus, even though there is still so much I don't know about it. I try not to complain when I get period pain. The gift I was so desperate to have I welcome each month. I am so thankful that I am now back in sync with the universal pull. However, I am hoping soon it will be put on hold so it can become the nourishing duvet for a growing soul. As I move through the aging process, I will endeavour to embrace and care for my human design that enables me to do the things that truly crafts my happiness. With these hands that assist in healing, and my encouraging mind that is now leading the way, I give thanks to my inner spark of God every day.

I start to reflect with gratitude and give thanks to the several teachers that have stepped me through my struggles. Many of them led, by their own battles, to their healing positions in this transforming time. As I review my labyrinth journey, I also thank my spiritual team, confirming to myself that they are not imaginary. I consider them as true friends. They continue to let me know there is still so much more going on behind the scenes. The labyrinth stencil I saw in the playground in my childhood now holds a special place in my heart as one of my early prompts. I also realised that the falling sensation I felt just before drifting off to sleep as a child can be mapped to the projection phenomenon. The colour my nana dyed her hair was the same colour linked to a higher chakra. Coincidence? Animals seem to be even more drawn to me with these new energies, confirming their level of communication through energy that is ever present. I am gaining so many answers to my childhood questions. Yet the more I learn, the more questions I have, so I continue to ask to be shown.

My desire to help others find parts of their labyrinth story became even stronger. I am pleased the process started even before I finished this story. A fellow healer, who also writes, was the person I asked to read my written text. Unfortunately, she was going away, so she referred me to a kind lady, a teacher, who was only too happy to help. I delivered my slightly unfinished first draft to her for review and she managed to read the first few chapters before heading out to a family engagement. To her amazement, this was the day that her young grandchild asked, "What is this stuff in my mouth?" A less dramatic investigation was required as she could calmly say that it was just spit, just as I had described from my childhood experience. On reading the rest of the chapters, she also found some other surprising similarities in experiences. Time prompts had been seen and a variety of these physical symptoms had also been experienced at certain times in her life. These associations could now be reflected on with a bit more depth to, hopefully, enjoy greater guidance.

In this present time, I acknowledge that my learnings here in this life will become part of my greater story. I begin to wonder if I would need to apply for certain positions on the other side. If I had to do up a résumé for God, what could I put in it? Would I embellish and say that my life has been all roses and smiles, or would I admit that I forgot to stop and smell the roses at times? I would sell the concept that my personal strength gained through my SPR (spiritual, physical restructure), and other life challenges, would enable me to bring immense compassion and unconditional love to my next role. I would also promise that I will continue to work for a mutually beneficial future.

I try to think what it would be like for spirit trying to wake us up so we can rise above the negative influences that weigh us down. I know they try to give us tools so we can overcome our limitations, helping us to mindfully choose a greater level of positive thought, which leads to progressive actions. I speculate that learning the art of dealing with frustration may be one of their key performance measures. I definitely need to give praise to my guiding team, as persistence was certainly one of their strengths. My wakeup has derailed my creative stalling train so I can move closer to my true innovative potential. Our creator's product range is so diverse that I don't think I could even comprehend all that there is. Hopefully, I get to climb the spiritual ladder to find out so I can continue to help co-create this miraculous adventure.

I now believe it to be true that the greater learning still continues through time and the timeless, so I am making it my goal to have no regrets. I will continue to dive deep to pull the plug on my doubts, by stilling my mind to assess what is true. I still have to check my thoughts before acting sometimes, to make sure my conduct fits the outcome I require. I had to laugh at myself when I started doing this, as on one occasion I did something that I had advised someone else not to do. If Dad were in the physical, I am sure he would have handed me his bogey keeper the other day.

I now start to take more notice of the beautiful things around me. On waking up one morning, the sun is shining through the trees outside. My snowflake crystal hanging from a window fastener splashes the room with the healing colours of grace. With a kiss from Kevin and a few morning giggles, I realise joy has come to join me. I am so grateful that this transformational experience occurred. My moon manifestation requests were granted, as I feel I have found my spiritual self. I have healed many wounds from my past, and I have found unconditional love by connecting with my divine. The more I connect to this level of unbounded love, it seems, the more I want to offer it to others.

I calmly appreciate the simple things in life, which seems to enhance each moment. Even when I hit a rough patch on my trail, I give value to the lesson—if it's mine or someone else's. I now dance and hug at the end of the group meditation evenings, and I embrace all I have learnt about our multidimensional universe. I will continue to follow my divine path led by love, and I have given myself the green light to integrate more fun along the way.

Rewards

Feeling a buzz,
An indescribable high,
A sense of belonging
Between Earth and our sky.

A reward from past
Or job well done,
To let your hair down
And just have some fun.

Be it dancing with friends
Or a gift that you're giving,
Touching one's heart
Is the purpose of living.

The purr from a cat
Or a stranger's smile,
Reading a poem,
Make them last for a while.

Good vibes to share,
It's infectious, you know.
You've got the green light,
So get in the flow.